ESSENTIAL MARY AUSTIN

ESSENTIAL MARY AUSTIN

A Selection of Mary Austin's Best Writing

Edited with an Introduction by
KEVIN HEARLE

Santa Clara University, Santa Clara, California
Heyday Books, Berkeley, California

Library of Congress Cataloging-in-Publication Data

Austin, Mary Hunter, 1868-1934.
  [Selections. 2006]
  Essential Mary Austin : a selection of Mary Austin's best writing / edited
with introduction by Kevin Hearle.
    p. cm.
  ISBN 1-59714-043-0 (pbk. : alk. paper)
  1. West (U.S.)--Literary collections. I. Austin, Mary Hunter, 1868-1934.
Land of little rain. II. Hearle, Kevin, 1958- III. Title.
  PS3501.U8A6 2006
  818'.5209--dc22
                                        2006017715

Cover Art and Design: Lorraine Rath
Interior Design: Philip Krayna, PKD, Berkeley
Typesetting: Lorraine Rath
Printing and Binding: McNaughton & Gunn, Saline, MI

Orders, inquiries, and correspondence should be addressed to:
    Heyday Books
    P. O. Box 9145, Berkeley, CA 94709
    (510) 549-3564, Fax (510) 549-1889
    www.heydaybooks.com

Printed in the United States of America

10 9 8 7 6 5 4 3 2 1

In memory of Josephine Schier Goodwin Hearle and Vera Hearle Reilly—two strong-willed, western women.

Contents

Acknowledgments

This book could not have been completed without the assistance of a number of wonderful people and institutions. I especially wish to express my gratitude for the generous financial support I received from The Book Club of California during my research for this book, and also my gratitude for the wonderful resources made available to me by The Huntington Library. Amazingly, the Huntington's dedicated staff is equal to its magnificent manuscript collections, and I would be remiss if I did not single out for thanks Sue Hodson, Curator of American Literary Manuscripts; William Deverell, Director of The Huntington Library/USC Center for the American West; and Suzi Krasnoo of Reader Services for their generosity of spirit.

I was singularly fortunate to be a participant in the seminar "The Redemptive West," put on by The Huntington Library and sponsored by the National Endowment for the Humanities in the summer of 2005. Although I came to that seminar with my ideas for this book already crystallized, it was a pleasure to be able to discuss my work with so many wonderful new colleagues. In particular, this book and I benefited from my discussions of Mary Austin with Nic Witschi of Western Michigan University, Cathryn Halverson of Kobe Women's University, and Bonney MacDonald of Union College. Dan Herman of Central Washington University also deserves special thanks for his willingness to play Virgil to my Dante through some difficult stretches of western U.S. historiography.

In the early phases of my research I was ably assisted by the staff of the Stanford University Libraries—especially the staff of the Department of Special Collections, Green Library—and by Beth Porter and Bill Michael of the Eastern California Museum.

Catherine Cocks of the School of American Research Press was of invaluable help to me in tracking down the current holders of Austin's various copyrights.

Finally, I am also grateful for the emotional support of a large group of friends and family. I have had the opportunity to edit this book only because Malcolm Margolin and Terry Beers believed in me. I have benefited from their support and that of the entire staff at Heyday Books. In particular, Jeannine Gendar, who stepped in to shepherd this book to press after my initial editor left to finish writing his own book, has been a calming influence. My wife, Libby, continues to support me in innumerable and unfathomable ways and to put up sweetly with my odd hours, my bookish pallor, and, for this book, my occasional forays into the desert. My younger brother, Michael, selflessly put me up in his apartment for a week while I was working at The Huntington Library. I thank them all. They have all helped to make this book what it is, and for that they deserve much credit. This book's faults, however, whatever they may prove to be, are not their responsibility. Above all, I am indebted to Mary Austin.

Introduction

During the first few decades of the twentieth century, there were many ways of discovering that Mary Hunter Austin was a remarkable woman. The simplest would probably have been to ask her. To her small-minded contemporaries, including her own mother and brother, that she was right about being remarkable only made it worse. She was read out of the Methodist Church for such offenses as giving baked goods to a Chinese man and consorting with Indians. She rejected her mother's opinion that her mentally handicapped daughter, Ruth, was God's judgment upon her as a mother. She taught school even though she was married. And she refused her mother's request that, if she had to write, she at least do it under a pseudonym.

Of course, if she hadn't been remarkable in exactly those ways that so infuriated and bewildered her mother and the good people of Inyo County as they constituted themselves one century ago, we probably would not know of Mary Austin today, much less be able to understand just how remarkable she truly was. She was born Mary Hunter in Carlinville, Illinois, in 1868. Her beloved father and much loved younger sister both died while Mary was still young, and her mother reacted to their deaths by putting all her hopes and pouring all her affection on her eldest son. She assumed that Mary's brother Jim would be a college man, but Mary had to battle her mother to get an education. As it was, Mary barely managed to complete a four-year degree from Carlinville's own Blackburn College in 1888—in a mere two and a half years—before her mother was moving the family to California because Jim wanted to homestead there.

Mary Hunter joined her family's migration west reluctantly, but it was in California that Mary Austin was born, and it was in California that she created herself as an author. In 1903, with the publication of *The Land of Little Rain*, she would become an overnight success; suddenly, after almost fifteen personally diffi-cult and outwardly unpromising years, she would be an acclaimed author.

Her first fortunate mistake along the path to that literary success was getting married. She married Stafford Wallace Austin in 1891, because her mother expected it. Wallace not only didn't support Mary's ambition to be a professional writer, he apparently didn't much care that she had opinions and ideas of her own. Despite all of his limitations, Wallace Austin did give one great gift to his bride. He gave her, however inadvertently, a new land, which she could bring to the English-speaking world through her writing. He dragged her to Independence and Lone Pine and Bishop, little towns, hoping—in those years when their water was still theirs—to become big ones. Outside the towns there were isolated mining camps, stagecoach stops, Shoshone and Paiute settlements, and prospectors' temporary diggings. In certain seasons sheep probably outnumbered people. Each kind of community had its own myths and tales for Mary Austin to collect and shape, but most of all, there was the land itself.

The core of Mary Austin's "land of little rain" is that amazing stretch of terrain where the dawn begins as a rosy glow on Mount Whitney's 14,494-foot peak, then turns golden as light illuminates granite across an assemblage of glaciated pinnacles, the Sierra Nevada towering over the long Owens Valley; this is Inyo County, where the sun's rising catches the flame-shaped bristlecone pines of the ancient White Mountains before igniting just another day of murderous heat at Badwater, in Death Valley. Austin's territory also includes the northern Mojave Desert, the yucca-studded Antelope Valley, the transverse Tehachapis, Rancho Tejon, the vast marshes of the lower San Joaquin Valley, and the Grapevine.

In that sparsely settled land, Mary Austin—feeling herself strand-ed and unappreciated—longed for a literary community. What she found instead, among the dispossessed and the self-exiled, were storytellers and teachers. Although she never learned to speak any American Indian languages, much of what Mary Austin knew of desert lore, and many of her tales, came from the Paiutes and the Shoshone. Her retellings of their myths and lore, especially the trickster tales, tend to miss completely both their humor and earthiness. At worst, her use of Shoshone and Paiute stories leaves her open to accusations of exploitation, and yet retroactive ethical judgments are rarely as simple as they initially seem. It is only fair to note in Mary Austin's defense that she wrote with great beauty and insight about lands and people that most of her contemporaries dismissed as being unworthy of serious contemplation. And having achieved fame, she was steadfast in using it to fight for the rights of American Indians to be first-rate Shoshones or Paiutes or Mojaves rather than second-rate whites.

Mary left her husband not long after *The Land of Little Rain* (reprinted here in its entirety) made her a best-selling author. She moved to Los Angeles for a time and was in San Francisco for the 1906 earthquake before moving to Carmel and helping to found that once glorious literary and artistic community. When Los Angeles completed its larcenous purchase of the water rights to the Owens River Valley (forcing the name change to the current Owens Valley), the Southern California Austin had loved became dead to her. She alternated between living in New York and Carmel, then traveled widely in Italy and England and across the United States.

She was a mystic with a degree in science, and a ferociously intelligent woman with the courage to live and write exceptionally. Her friends included Teddy Roosevelt (after his presidency); novelists Jack London, Sinclair Lewis, H. G. Wells, Joseph Conrad, and Willa Cather; poets William Butler Yeats, Robinson Jeffers, George Sterling, and Robert Frost; playwright George Bernard Shaw; and other prominent personalities of the day, including Isadora Duncan, Emma Goldman, Mabel Dodge Luhan, and William James. Her acquaintances included W. E. B. DuBois, D. H. Lawrence, Countee Cullen, James Weldon Johnson, and a host of other names now no longer well known. And yet, celebrity itself didn't much interest her. In *Earth Horizon* (represented here by a brief selection describing the culture of the Mojave stagecoach), her autobiography, she describes her first trip to visit Joseph Conrad thusly: "Herbert drove me." Herbert's last name was Hoover.

After the publication of *The Land of Little Rain*, Mary Austin was a famous author for the rest of her life. Before her death in 1934, she wrote more than thirty books (how many depends upon how you count a few books that were rewritten, expanded, or excerpted from previously published books). She won the Pulitzer Prize for drama with a play, *The Arrow-Maker*, which now seems terribly dated. She also wrote a guide to political participation for newly enfranchised women voters; wonderful short story collections for adults and children (including *Lost Borders*, from which three stories are reprinted here in their entirety); retellings of American Indian poetry and myths; travel guides to California and to Arizona and New Mexico; a study of California sheep lore (*The Flock*, which is represented here by significant selections from two chapters); various books on Jesus and spiritual topics; a book on race and the nature of human talent which, though reflective of the thinking of her day, is deeply troubling; a romance of Spanish California; a woodland fantasy set near Carmel; an ambitious but awkwardly constructed novel of the conflict between small farmers and big money in turn-of-the-century California (*The Ford*, which is represented here by excerpts from two chapters); and a variety of social novels whose settings include a California college town, backstage Chicago and New York, a small Midwestern town, Italy, the California desert, the mountains of New Mexico, and muckraking circles in New York.

Austin's consistent themes are the role of women in society, and the absolute necessity for aesthetics and culture to be based on the physical environment. Her best work along those themes still rewards attention. Her best fiction is peopled with remarkable women shaped by, and reacting to, western society and landscape, and ordinary women stunted by the pressures of small town conformity. Her women and her men alike are bowed by the weight of their spouses' and neighbors' expectations, or by their own unmet hopes. Her best structured, least sentimental, and most poetic novel, *Cactus Thorn*, (the first chapter of which is reprinted here in its entirety) was never published in her lifetime, but we are fortunate to have it now. Of her body of work as a whole, perhaps the best judgment we can make—in the midst of the current, well-deserved renewal of critical interest in Austin—paraphrases what she herself wrote about her friend the poet George Sterling: whatever place in American literature she will finally take—if not the highest, it will surely not be a low one—Austin herself will become a myth there, a figure of a woman noble, inconsequent, but never utterly denied her desire to identify herself with truth and beauty. Even there, I have to quibble with "inconsequent," but don't take my word for it. Take those of hers that follow, and judge for yourself.

The Land of Little Rain

Preface

I confess to a great liking for the Indian fashion of name-giving: every man known by that phrase which best expresses him to whoso names him. Thus he may be Mighty-Hunter, or Man-Afraid-of-a-Bear, according as he is called by friend or enemy, and Scar-Face to those who knew him by the eye's grasp only. No other fashion, I think, sets so well with the various natures that inhabit in us, and if you agree with me you will understand why so few names are written here as they appear in the geography. For if I love a lake known by the name of the man who discovered it, which endears itself by reason of the close-locked pines it nourishes about its borders, you may look in my account to find it so described. But if the Indians have been there before me, you shall have their name, which is always beautifully fit and does not originate in the poor human desire for perpetuity.

Nevertheless there are certain peaks, cañons, and clear meadow spaces which are above all compassing of words, and have a certain fame as of the nobly great to whom we give no familiar names. Guided by these you may reach my country and find or not find, according as it lieth in you, much that is set down here. And more. The earth is no wanton to give up all her best to every comer, but keeps a sweet, separate intimacy for each. But if you do not find it all as I write, think me not less dependable nor yourself less clever. There is a sort of pretense allowed in matters of the heart, as one should say by way of illustration, "I know a man who...," and so give up his dearest experience without betrayal. And I am in no mind to direct you to delectable places toward which you will hold yourself less tenderly than I. So by this fashion of naming I keep

faith with the land and annex to my own estate a very great territory to which none has a surer title.

The country where you may have sight and touch of that which
is written lies between the high Sierras south from Yosemite—east
and south over a very great assemblage of broken ranges beyond
Death Valley, and on illimitably into the Mojave Desert. You may
come into the borders of it from the south by a stage journey that
has the effect of involving a great lapse of time, or from the north
by rail, dropping out of the overland route at Reno. The best of all
ways is over the Sierra passes by pack and trail, seeing and believ-
ing. But the real heart and core of the country are not to be come at
in a month's vacation. One must summer and winter with the land
and wait its occasions. Pine woods that take two and three seasons
to the ripening of cones, roots that lie by in the sand seven years
awaiting a growing rain, firs that grow fifty years before flowering,—these do not scrape acquaintance. But if ever you come
beyond the borders as far as the town that lies in a hill dimple at the
foot of Kearsarge, never leave it until you have knocked at the door
of the brown house under the willow-tree at the end of the village
street, and there you shall have such news of the land, of its trails
and what is astir in them, as one lover of it can give to another.

The Land of Little Rain

East away from the Sierras, south from Panamint and Amargosa, east and south many an uncounted mile, is the Country of Lost Borders.

Ute, Paiute, Mojave, and Shoshone inhabit its frontiers, and as far into the heart of it as a man dare go. Not the law, but the land sets the limit. Desert is the name it wears upon the maps, but the Indian's is the better word. Desert is a loose term to indicate land that supports no man; whether the land can be bitted and broken to that purpose is not proven. Void of life it never is, however dry the air and villainous the soil.

This is the nature of that country. There are hills, rounded, blunt, burned, squeezed up out of chaos, chrome and vermilion painted, aspiring to the snow-line. Between the hills lie high level-looking plains full of intolerable sun glare, or narrow valleys drowned in a blue haze. The hill surface is streaked with ash drift and black, unweathered lava flows. After rains water accumulates in the hollows of small closed valleys, and, evaporating, leaves hard dry levels of pure desertness that get the local name of dry lakes. Where the mountains are steep and the rains heavy, the pool is never quite dry, but dark and bitter, rimmed about with the efflorescence of alkaline deposits. A thin crust of it lies along the marsh over the vegetating area, which has neither beauty nor freshness. In the broad wastes open to the wind the sand drifts in hummocks about the stubby shrubs, and between them the soil shows saline traces. The sculpture of the hills here is more wind than water work, though the quick storms do sometimes scar them past many a year's redeeming. In all the Western desert edges there are essays in miniature at the famed, terrible Grand Cañon, to which, if you keep on long enough in this country, you will come at last.

Since this is a hill country one expects to find springs, but not to depend upon them; for when found they are often brackish and unwholesome, or maddening, slow dribbles in a thirsty soil. Here you find the hot sink of Death Valley, or high rolling districts where the air has always a tang of frost. Here are the long heavy winds and breathless calms on the tilted mesas where dust devils dance, whirling up into a wide, pale sky. Here you have no rain when all the earth cries for it, or quick downpours called cloudbursts for violence. A land of lost rivers, with little in it to love; yet a land that once visited must be come back to inevitably. If it were not so there would be little told of it.

This is the country of three seasons. From June on to November it lies hot, still, and unbearable, sick with violent unrelieving storms; then on until April, chill, quiescent, drinking its scant rain and scanter snows; from April to the hot season again, blossoming, radiant, and seductive. These months are only approximate; later or earlier the rain-laden wind may drift up the water gate of the Colorado from the Gulf, and the land sets its seasons by the rain.

The desert floras shame us with their cheerful adaptations to the seasonal limitations. Their whole duty is to flower and fruit, and they do it hardly, or with tropical luxuriance, as the rain admits. It is recorded in the report of the Death Valley expedition that after a year of abundant rains, on the Colorado desert was found a specimen of Amaranthus ten feet high. A year later the same species in the same place matured in the drought at four inches. One hopes the land may breed like qualities in her human offspring, not tritely to "try," but to do. Seldom does the desert herb attain the full stature of the type. Extreme aridity and extreme altitude have the same dwarfing effect, so that we find in the high Sierras and in Death Valley related species in miniature that reach a comely growth in mean temperatures. Very fertile are the desert plants in expedients to prevent evaporation, turning their foliage edgewise toward the sun, growing silky hairs, exuding viscid gum. The wind, which has a long sweep, harries and helps them. It rolls up dunes about the stocky stems, encompassing and protective, and above the dunes, which may be, as with the mesquite, three times as high as a man, the blossoming twigs flourish and bear fruit.

There are many areas in the desert where drinkable water lies within a few feet of the surface, indicated by the mesquite and the bunch grass (*Sporobolus airoides*). It is this nearness of unimagined help that makes the tragedy of desert deaths. It is related that the final breakdown of that hapless party that gave Death Valley its forbidding name occurred in a locality where shallow wells would have saved them. But how were they to know that? Properly equipped it is possible to go safely across that ghastly sink, yet every year it takes its toll of death, and yet men find there sun-dried mummies, of whom no trace or recollection is preserved. To underestimate one's thirst, to pass a given landmark to the right or left, to find a dry spring where one looked for running water—there is no help for any of these things.

Along springs and sunken watercourses one is surprised to find such water-loving plants as grow widely in moist ground, but the true desert breeds its own kind, each in its particular habitat. The angle of the slope, the frontage of a hill, the structure of the soil determines the plant. South-looking hills are nearly bare, and the lower tree-line higher here by a thousand feet. Cañons running east and west will have one wall naked and one clothed. Around dry lakes and marshes the herbage preserves a set and orderly arrangement. Most species have well-defined areas of growth, the best index the voiceless land can give the traveler of his whereabouts.

If you have any doubt about it, know that the desert begins with the creosote. This immortal shrub spreads down into Death Valley and up to the lower timber-line, odorous and medicinal as you might guess from the name, wandlike, with shining fretted foliage. Its vivid green is grateful to the eye in a wilderness of gray and greenish white shrubs. In the spring it exudes a resinous gum which the Indians of those parts know how to use with pulverized rock for cementing arrow points to shafts. Trust Indians not to miss any virtues of the plant world!

Nothing the desert produces expresses it better than the unhappy growth of the tree yuccas. Tormented, thin forests of it stalk

drearily in the high mesas, particularly in that triangular slip that
fans out eastward from the meeting of the Sierras and coastwise
hills where the first swings across the southern end of the San
Joaquin Valley. The yucca bristles with bayonet-pointed leaves,
dull green, growing shaggy with age, tipped with panicles of fetid,
greenish bloom. After death, which is slow, the ghostly hollow net-
work of its woody skeleton, with hardly power to rot, makes the
moonlight fearful. Before the yucca has come to flower, while yet
its bloom is a creamy cone-shaped bud of the size of a small cab-
bage, full of sugary sap, the Indians twist it deftly out of its fence of
daggers and roast it for their own delectation. So it is that in those
parts where man inhabits one sees young plants of *Yucca arborensis*
infrequently. Other yuccas, cacti, low herbs, a thousand sorts, one
finds journeying east from the coastwise hills. There is neither
poverty of soil nor species to account for the sparseness of desert
growth, but simply that each plant requires more room. So much
earth must be preempted to extract so much moisture. The real
struggle for existence, the real brain of the plant, is underground;
above there is room for a rounded perfect growth. In Death Valley,
reputed the very core of desolation, are nearly two hundred identi-
fied species.

Above the lower tree-line, which is also the snow-line, mapped
out abruptly by the sun, one finds spreading growth of piñon,
juniper, branched nearly to the ground, lilac and sage, and scattering white pines.

There is no special preponderance of self-fertilized or wind-
fertilized plants, but everywhere the demand for and evidence of
insect life. Now where there are seeds and insects there will be birds
and small mammals, and where these are, will come the slinking,
sharp-toothed kind that prey on them. Go as far as you dare in the
heart of a lonely land, you cannot go so far that life and death are
not before you. Painted lizards slip in and out of rock crevices, and
pant on the white hot sands. Birds, hummingbirds even, nest in the
cactus scrub; woodpeckers befriend the demoniac yuccas; out of the
stark, treeless waste rings the music of the night-singing mocking-
bird. If it be summer and the sun well down, there will be a burrowing owl to call. Strange, furry, tricksy things dart across the
open places, or sit motionless in the conning towers of the creosote.

The poet may have "named all the birds without a gun," but not the fairy-footed, ground-inhabiting, furtive, small folk of the rainless regions. They are too many and too swift; how many you would not believe without seeing the footprint tracings in the sand. They are nearly all night workers, finding the days too hot and white. In mid-desert where there are no cattle, there are no birds of carrion, but if you go far in that direction the chances are that you will find yourself shadowed by their tilted wings. Nothing so large as a man can move unspied upon in that country, and they know well how the land deals with strangers. There are hints to be had here of the way in which a land forces new habits on its dwellers. The quick increase of suns at the end of spring sometimes overtakes birds in their nesting and effects a reversal of the ordinary manner of incubation. It becomes necessary to keep eggs cool rather than warm. One hot, stifling spring in the Little Antelope I had occasion to pass and repass frequently the nest of a pair of meadowlarks, located unhappily in the shelter of a very slender weed. I never caught them sitting except near night, but at midday they stood, or drooped above it, half fainting with pitifully parted bills, between their treasure and the sun. Sometimes both of them together with wings spread and half lifted continued a spot of shade in a temperature that constrained me at last in a fellow feeling to spare them a bit of canvas for permanent shelter. There was a fence in that country shutting in a cattle range, and along its fifteen miles of posts one could be sure of finding a bird or two in every strip of shadow; sometimes the sparrow and the hawk, with wings trailed and beaks parted, drooping in the white truce of noon.

If one is inclined to wonder at first how so many dwellers came to be in the loneliest land that ever came out of God's hands, what they do there and why stay, one does not wonder so much after having lived there. None other than this long brown land lays such a hold on the affections. The rainbow hills, the tender bluish mists, the luminous radiance of the spring, have the lotus charm. They trick the sense of time, so that once inhabiting there you always mean to go away without quite realizing that you have not done it. Men who have lived there, miners and cattle-men, will tell you this, not so fluently, but emphatically, cursing the land and going back to it. For one thing there is the divinest, cleanest air to be breathed anywhere in God's world. Some day the world will understand that, and the little oases on the windy tops of hills will harbor for healing its ailing, house-weary broods. There is promise there of great wealth in ores and earths, which is no wealth by reason of being so far removed from water and workable conditions, but men are bewitched by it and tempted to try the impossible.

You should hear Salty Williams tell how he used to drive eighteen and twenty-mule teams from the borax marsh to Mojave, ninety miles, with the trail wagon full of water barrels. Hot days the mules would go so mad for drink that the clank of the water bucket set them into an uproar of hideous, maimed noises, and a tangle of harness chains, while Salty would sit on the high seat with the sun glare heavy in his eyes, dealing out curses of pacification in a level, uninterested voice until the clamor fell off from sheer exhaustion. There was a line of shallow graves along that road; they used to count on dropping a man or two of every new gang of coolies brought out in the hot season. But when he lost his swamper, smitten without warning at the noon halt, Salty quit his job; he said it was "too durn hot." The swamper he buried by the way with stones upon him to keep the coyotes from digging him up, and seven years later I read the penciled lines on the pine headboard, still bright and unweathered.

But before that, driving up on the Mojave stage, I met Salty again crossing Indian Wells, his face from the high seat, tanned and ruddy as a harvest moon, looming through the golden dust above his eighteen mules. The land had called him.

The palpable sense of mystery in the desert air breeds fables, chiefly of lost treasure. Somewhere within its stark borders, if one believes report, is a hill strewn with nuggets; one seamed with virgin silver; an old clayey water-bed where Indians scooped up earth to make cooking pots and shaped them reeking with grains of pure gold. Old miners drifting about the desert edges, weathered into the semblance of the tawny hills, will tell you tales like these convincingly. After a little sojourn in that land you will believe them on their own account. It is a question whether it is not better to be bitten by the little horned snake of the desert that goes sidewise and strikes without coiling, than by the tradition of a lost mine.

And yet—and yet—is it not perhaps to satisfy expectation that one falls into the tragic key in writing of desertness? The more you wish of it the more you get, and in the mean time lose much of pleasantness. In that country which begins at the foot of the east slope of the Sierras and spreads out by less and less lofty hill ranges toward the Great Basin, it is possible to live with great zest, to have red blood and delicate joys, to pass and repass about one's daily performance an area that would make an Atlantic seaboard State, and that with no peril, and, according to our way of thought, no particular difficulty. At any rate, it was not people who went into the desert merely to write it up who invented the fabled Hassaympa, of whose waters, if any drink, they can no more see fact as naked fact, but all radiant with the color of romance. I, who must have drunk of it in my twice seven years' wanderings, am assured that it is worth while.

For all the toil the desert takes of a man it gives compensations, deep breaths, deep sleep, and the communion of the stars. It comes upon one with new force in the pauses of the night that the Chaldeans were a desert-bred people. It is hard to escape the sense of mastery as the stars move in the wide clear heavens to risings and settings unobscured. They look large and near and palpitant; as if they moved on some stately service not needful to declare. Wheeling to their stations in the sky, they make the poor world-fret of no account. Of no account you who lie out there watching, nor the lean coyote that stands off in the scrub from you and howls and howls.

Water Trails of the Ceriso

By the end of the dry season the water trails of the Ceriso are worn to a white ribbon in the leaning grass, spread out faint and fanwise toward the homes of gopher and ground rat and squirrel. But however faint to man-sight, they are sufficiently plain to the furred and feathered folk who travel them. Getting down to the eye level of rat and squirrel kind, one perceives what might easily be wide and winding roads to us if they occurred in thick plantations of trees three times the height of a man. It needs but a slender thread of barrenness to make a mouse trail in the forest of the sod. To the little people the water trails are as country roads, with scents as signboards.

It seems that man-height is the least fortunate of all heights from which to study trails. It is better to go up the front of some tall hill, say the spur of Black Mountain, looking back and down across the hollow of the Ceriso. Strange how long the soil keeps the impression of any continuous treading, even after grass has overgrown it. Twenty years since, a brief heyday of mining at Black Mountain made a stage road across the Ceriso, yet the parallel lines that are the wheel traces show from the height dark and well defined. Afoot in the Ceriso one looks in vain for any sign of it. So all the paths that wild creatures use going down to the Lone Tree Spring are mapped out whitely from this level, which is also the level of the hawks.

There is little water in the Ceriso at the best of times, and that little brackish and smelling vilely, but by a lone juniper where the rim of the Ceriso breaks away to the lower country, there is a perpetual rill of fresh sweet drink in the midst of lush grass and watercress. In the dry season there is no water else for a man's long journey of a day. East to the foot of Black Mountain, and north and south without counting, are the burrows of small rodents, rat and squirrel kind. Under the sage are the shallow forms of the jack-rabbits, and in the dry banks of washes, and among the strewn fragments of black rock, lairs of bobcat, fox, and coyote.

The coyote is your true water-witch, one who snuffs and paws, snuffs and paws again at the smallest spot of moisture-scented earth until he has freed the blind water from the soil. Many water-holes are no more than this detected by the lean hobo of the hills in localities where not even an Indian would look for it.

It is the opinion of many wise and busy people that the hill-folk pass the ten-month interval between the end and renewal of winter rains, with no drink; but your true idler, with days and nights to spend beside the water trails, will not subscribe to it. The trails begin, as I said, very far back in the Ceriso, faintly, and converge in one span broad, white, hard-trodden way in the gully of the spring. And why trails if there are no travelers in that direction?

I have yet to find the land not scarred by the thin, far roadways of rabbits and what not of furry folks that run in them. Venture to look for some seldom-touched water-hole, and so long as the trails run with your general direction make sure you are right, but if they begin to cross yours at never so slight an angle, to converge toward a point left or right of your objective, no matter what the maps say, or your memory, trust them; they *know*.

It is very still in the Ceriso by day, so that were it not for the evidence of those white beaten ways, it might be the desert it looks. The sun is hot in the dry season, and the days are filled with the glare of it. Now and again some unseen coyote signals his pack in a long-drawn, dolorous whine that comes from no determinate point, but nothing stirs much before mid-afternoon. It is a sign when there begin to be hawks skimming above the sage that the little people are going about their business.

We have fallen on a very careless usage, speaking of wild creatures as if they were bound by some such limitation as hampers clockwork. When we say of one and another, they are night prowlers, it is perhaps true only as the things they feed upon are more easily come by in the dark, and they know well how to adjust themselves to conditions wherein food is more plentiful by day. And their accustomed performance is very much a matter of keen eye, keener scent, quick ear, and a better memory of sights and sounds than man dares boast. Watch a coyote come out of his lair and cast about in his mind where he will go for his daily killing. You cannot very well tell what decides him, but very easily that he has decided. He trots or breaks into short gallops, with very perceptible pauses to look up and about at landmarks, alters his tack a little, looking forward and back to steer his proper course. I am persuaded that the coyotes in my valley, which is narrow and beset with steep, sharp hills, in long passages steer by the pinnacles of the sky-line, going with head cocked to one side to keep to the left or right of such and such a promontory.

I have trailed a coyote often, going across country, perhaps to where some slant-winged scavenger hanging in the air signaled prospect of a dinner, and found his track such as a man, a very intelligent man accustomed to a hill country, and a little cautious, would make to the same point. Here a detour to avoid a stretch of too little cover, there a pause on the rim of a gully to pick the better way,—and it is usually the best way,—and making his point with the greatest economy of effort. Since the time of Seyavi the deer have shifted their feeding ground across the valley at the beginning of deep snows, by way of the Black Rock, fording the river at Charley's Butte, and making straight for the mouth of the cañon that is the easiest going to the winter pastures on Waban. So they still cross, though whatever trail they had has been long broken by ploughed ground; but from the mouth of Tinpah Creek, where the deer come out of the Sierras, it is easily seen that the creek, the point of Black Rock, and Charley's Butte are in line with the wide bulk of shade that is the foot of Waban Pass. And along with this the deer have learned that Charley's Butte is almost the only possible ford, and all the shortest crossing of the valley. It seems that the wild creatures have learned all that is important to their way of life except the changes of the moon. I have seen some prowling fox or coyote, surprised by its sudden rising from behind the mountain wall, slink in its increasing glow, watch it furtively from the cover of near-by brush, unprepared and half uncertain of its identity until it rode clear of the peaks, and finally make off with all the air of one caught napping by an ancient joke. The moon in its wanderings must be a sort of exasperation to cunning beasts, likely to spoil by untimely risings some fore-planned mischief.

But to take the trail again; the coyotes that are astir in the Ceriso of late afternoons, harrying the rabbits from their shallow forms, and the hawks that sweep and swing above them, are not there from any mechanical promptings of instinct, but because they know of old experience that the small fry are about to take to seed gathering and the water trails. The rabbits begin it, taking the trail with long, light leaps, one eye and ear cocked to the hills from whence a coyote might descend upon them at any moment. Rabbits are a foolish people. They do not fight except with their own kind, nor use their paws except for feet, and appear to have no reason for existence but to furnish meals for meat-eaters. In flight they seem to rebound from the earth of their own elasticity, but keep a sober pace going to the spring. It is the young watercress that tempts them and the pleasures of society, for they seldom drink. Even in localities where there are flowing streams they seem to prefer the moisture that collects on herbage, and after rains may be seen rising on their haunches to drink delicately the clear drops caught in the tops of the young sage. But drink they must, as I have often seen them mornings and evenings at the rill that goes by my door. Wait long enough at the Lone Tree Spring and sooner or later they will all come in. But here their matings are accomplished, and though they are fearful of so little as a cloud shadow or blown leaf, they contrive to have some playful hours. At the spring the bobcat drops down upon them from the black rock, and the red fox picks them up returning in the dark. By day the hawk and eagle overshadow them, and the coyote has all times and seasons for his own.

Cattle, when there are any in the Ceriso, drink morning and evening, spending the night on the warm last lighted slopes of neighboring hills, stirring with the peep o' day. In these half wild spotted steers the habits of an earlier lineage persist. It must be long since they have made beds for themselves, but before lying down they turn themselves round and round as dogs do. They choose bare and stony ground, exposed fronts of westward facing hills, and lie down in companies. Usually by the end of the summer the cattle have been driven or gone of their own choosing to the mountain meadows. One year a maverick yearling, strayed or overlooked by the vaqueros, kept on until the season's end, and so betrayed another visitor to the spring that else I might have missed. On a certain morning the half-eaten carcass lay at the foot of the black rock, and in moist earth by the rill of the spring, the foot-pads of a cougar, puma, mountain lion, or whatever the beast is rightly called. The kill must have been made early in the evening, for it appeared that the cougar had been twice to the spring; and since the meat-eater drinks little until he has eaten, he must have fed and drunk, and after an interval of lying up in the black rock, had eaten and drunk again. There was no knowing how far he had come, but if he came again the second night he found that the coyotes had left him very little of his kill.

Nobody ventures to say how infrequently and at what hour the small fry visit the spring. There are such numbers of them that if each came once between the last of spring and the first of winter rains, there would still be water trails. I have seen badgers drinking about the hour when the light takes on the yellow tinge it has from coming slantwise through the hills. They find out shallow places, and are loath to wet their feet. Rats and chipmunks have been observed visiting the spring as late as nine o'clock mornings. The larger spermophiles that live near the spring and keep awake to work all day, come and go at no particular hour, drinking sparingly. At long intervals on half-lighted days, meadow and field mice steal delicately along the trail. These visitors are all too small to be watched carefully at night, but for evidence of their frequent coming there are the trails that may be traced miles out among the crisping grasses. On rare nights, in the places where no grass grows between the shrubs, and the sand silvers whitely to the moon, one sees them whisking to and fro on innumerable errands of seed gathering, but the chief witnesses of their presence near the spring are the elf owls. Those burrow-haunting, speckled fluffs of greediness begin a twilight flitting toward the spring, feeding as they go on grasshoppers, lizards, and small, swift creatures, diving into burrows to catch field mice asleep, battling with chipmunks at their own doors, and getting down in great numbers toward the lone juniper. Now owls do not love water greatly on its own account. Not to my knowledge have I caught one drinking or bathing, though on night wanderings across the mesa they flit up from under the horse's feet along stream borders. Their presence near the spring in great numbers would indicate the presence of the things they feed upon. All night the rustle and soft hooting keeps on in the neighborhood of the spring, with seldom small shrieks of mortal agony. It is clear day before they have all gotten back to their particular hummocks, and if one follows cautiously, not to frighten them into some near-by burrow, it is possible to trail them far up the slope.

The crested quail that troop in the Ceriso are the happiest frequenters of the water trails. There is no furtiveness about their morning drink. About the time the burrowers and all that feed upon them are addressing themselves to sleep, great flocks pour down the trails with that peculiar melting motion of moving quail, twittering, shoving, and shouldering. They splatter into the shallows, drink daintily, shake out small showers over their perfect coats, and melt away again into the scrub, preening and pranking, with soft contented noises.

After the quail, sparrows and ground-inhabiting birds bathe with the utmost frankness and a great deal of splutter; and here in the heart of noon hawks resort, sitting panting, with wings aslant, and a truce to all hostilities because of the heat. One summer there came a road-runner up from the lower valley, peeking and prying, and he had never any patience with the water baths of the sparrows. His own ablutions were performed in the clean, hopeful dust of the chaparral; and whenever he happened on their morning splatterings, he would depress his glossy crest, slant his shining tail to the level of his body, until he looked most like some bright venomous snake, daunting them with shrill abuse and feint of battle. Then suddenly he would go tilting and balancing down the gully in fine disdain, only to return in a day or two to make sure the foolish bodies were still at it.

Out on the Ceriso about five miles, and wholly out of sight of it, near where the immemorial foot trail goes up from Saline Flat toward Black Mountain, is a water sign worth turning out of the trail to see. It is a laid circle of stones large enough not to be disturbed by any ordinary hap, with an opening flanked by two parallel rows of similar stones, between which were

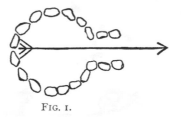

FIG. I.

an arrow placed, touching the opposite rim of the circle, thus (Fig. I), it would point as the crow flies to the spring. It is the old, indubitable water mark of the Shoshones. One still finds it in the desert ranges in Salt Wells and Mesquite valleys, and along the slopes of Waban. On the other side of Ceriso, where the black rock begins, about a mile from the spring, is the work of an older, forgotten people. The rock hereabout is all volcanic, fracturing with a crystalline whitish surface, but weathered outside to furnace blackness. Around the spring, where must have been a gathering place of the tribes, it is scored over with strange pictures and symbols that have no meaning to the Indians of the present day; but out where the rock begins, there is carved into the white heart of it a

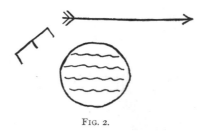

FIG. 2.

pointing arrow over the symbol for distance and a circle full of wavy lines (Fig. 2) reading thus: "In this direction three [units of measurement unknown] is a spring of sweet water; look for it."

The Scavengers

Fifty-seven buzzards, one on each of fifty-seven fence posts at the rancho El Tejon, on a mirage-breeding September morning, sat solemnly while the white tilted travelers' vans lumbered down the Canada de los Uvas. After three hours they had only clapped their wings, or exchanged posts. The season's end in the vast dim valley of the San Joaquin is palpitatingly hot, and the air breathes like cotton wool. Through it all the buzzards sit on the fences and low hummocks, with wings spread fanwise for air. There is no end to them, and they smell to heaven. Their heads droop, and all their communication is a rare, horrid croak.

The increase of wild creatures is in proportion to the things they feed upon: the more carrion the more buzzards. The end of the third successive dry year bred them beyond belief. The first year quail mated sparingly; the second year the wild oats matured no seed; the third, cattle died in their tracks with their heads towards the stopped watercourses. And that year the scavengers were as black as the plague all across the mesa and up the treeless, tumbled hills. On clear days they betook themselves to the upper air, where they hung motionless for hours. That year there were vultures among them, distinguished by the white patches under the wings. All their offensiveness notwithstanding, they have a stately flight. They must also have what pass for good qualities among themselves, for they are social, not to say clannish.

It is a very squalid tragedy,—that of the dying brutes and the scavenger birds. Death by starvation is slow. The heavy-headed, rack-boned cattle totter in the fruitless trails; they stand for long,

patient intervals; they lie down and do not rise. There is fear in
their eyes when they are first stricken, but afterward only intolerable weariness. I suppose the dumb creatures know nearly as much
of death as do their betters, who have only the more imagination.
Their even-breathing submission after the first agony is their trib-
ute to its inevitableness. It needs a nice discrimination to say which
of the basket-ribbed cattle is likest to afford the next meal, but the
scavengers make few mistakes. One stoops to the quarry and the
flock follows.

Cattle once down may be days in dying. They stretch out their
necks along the ground, and roll up their slow eyes at longer intervals. The buzzards have all the time, and no beak is dropped or
talon struck until the breath is wholly passed. It is doubtless the
economy of nature to have the scavengers by to clean up the carrion, but a wolf at the throat would be a shorter agony than the long
stalking and sometime perchings of these loathsome watchers.
Suppose now it were a man in this long-drawn, hungrily spied upon
distress! When Timmie O'Shea was lost on Armogossa Flats for
three days without water, Long Tom Basset found him, not by any
trail, but by making straight away for the points where he saw buzzards stooping. He could hear the beat of their wings, Tom said, and
trod on their shadows, but O'Shea was past recalling what he
thought about things after the second day. My friend Ewan told
me, among other things, when he came back from San Juan Hill,
that not all the carnage of battle turned his bowels as the sight of
slant black wings rising flockwise before the burial squad.

There are three kinds of noises buzzards make,—it is impossible
to call them notes,—raucous and elemental. There is a short croak
of alarm, and the same syllable in a modified tone to serve all the
purposes of ordinary conversation. The old birds make a kind of
throaty chuckling to their young, but if they have any love song I
have not heard it. The young yawp in the nest a little, with more
breath than noise. It is seldom one finds a buzzard's nest, seldom
that grown-ups find a nest of any sort; it is only children to whom
these things happen by right. But by making a business of it one
may come upon them in wide, quiet cañons, or on the lookouts of
lonely, table-topped mountains, three or four together, in the tops of

stubby trees or on rotten cliffs well open to the sky.

It is probable that the buzzard is gregarious, but it seems unlikely from the small number of young noted at any time that every female incubates each year. The young birds are easily distinguished by their size when feeding, and high up in air by the worn primaries of the older birds. It is when the young go out of the nest on their first foraging that the parents, full of a crass and simple pride, make their indescribable chucklings of gobbling, gluttonous delight. The little ones would be amusing as they tug and tussle, if one could forget what it is they feed upon.

One never comes any nearer to the vulture's nest or nestlings than hearsay. They keep to the southerly Sierras, and are bold enough, it seems, to do killing on their own account when no carrion is at hand. They dog the shepherd from camp to camp, the hunter home from the hill, and will even carry away offal from under his hand.

The vulture merits respect for his bigness and for his bandit airs, but he is a sombre bird, with none of the buzzard's frank satisfaction in his offensiveness.

The least objectionable of the inland scavengers is the raven, frequenter of the desert ranges, the same called locally "carrion crow." He is handsomer and has such an air. He is nice in his habits and is said to have likable traits. A tame one in a Shoshone camp was the butt of much sport and enjoyed it. He could all but talk and was another with the children, but an arrant thief. The raven will eat most things that come his way,—eggs and young of ground-nesting birds, seeds even, lizards and grasshoppers, which he catches cleverly; and whatever he is about, let a coyote trot never so softly by, the raven flaps up and after; for whatever the coyote can pull down or nose out is meat also for the carrion crow.

And never a coyote comes out of his lair for killing, in the country of the carrion crows, but looks up first to see where they may be gathering. It is a sufficient occupation for a windy morning, on the lineless, level mesa, to watch the pair of them eying each other furtively, with a tolerable assumption of unconcern, but no doubt with a certain amount of good understanding about it. Once at Red Rock, in a year of green pasture, which is a bad time for the scavengers, we saw two buzzards, five ravens, and a coyote feeding on the same carrion, and only the coyote seemed ashamed of the company.

Probably we never fully credit the interdependence of wild creatures, and their cognizance of the affairs of their own kind. When the five coyotes that range the Tejon from Pasteria to Tunawai planned a relay race to bring down an antelope strayed from the band, beside myself to watch, an eagle swung down from Mt. Pinos, buzzards materialized out of invisible ether, and hawks came trooping like small boys to a street fight. Rabbits sat up in the chaparral and cocked their ears, feeling themselves quite safe for the once as the hunt swung near them. Nothing happens in the deep wood that the blue jays are not all agog to tell. The hawk follows the badger, the coyote the carrion crow, and from their aerial stations the buzzards watch each other. What would be worth knowing is how much of their neighbor's affairs the new generations learn for themselves, and how much they are taught of their elders.

So wide is the range of the scavengers that it is never safe to say, eyewitness to the contrary, that there are few or many in such a place. Where the carrion is, there will the buzzards be gathered together, and in three days' journey you will not sight another one. The way up from Mojave to Red Butte is all desertness, affording no pasture and scarcely a rill of water. In a year of little rain in the south, flocks and herds were driven to the number of thousands along this road to the perennial pastures of the high ranges. It is a long, slow trail, ankle deep in bitter dust that gets up in the slow wind and moves along the backs of the crawling cattle. In the worst of times one in three will pine and fall out by the way. In the defiles of Red Rock, the sheep piled up a stinking lane; it was the sun smiting by day. To these shambles came buzzards, vultures, and coyotes from all the country round, so that on the Tejon, the Ceriso, and the Little Antelope there were not scavengers enough to keep the country clean. All that summer the dead mummified in the open or dropped slowly back to earth in the quagmires of the bitter springs. Meanwhile from Red Rock to Coyote Holes, and from Coyote Holes to Haiwai the scavengers gorged and gorged.

The coyote is not a scavenger by choice, preferring his own kill, but being on the whole a lazy dog, is apt to fall into carrion eating because it is easier. The red fox and bobcat, a little pressed by hunger, will eat of any other animal's kill, but will not ordinarily touch what dies of itself, and are exceedingly shy of food that has been manhandled.

Very clean and handsome, quite belying his relationship in appearance, is Clark's crow, that scavenger and plunderer of mountain camps. It is permissible to call him by his common name, "Camp Robber:" he has earned it. Not content with refuse, he pecks open meal sacks, filches whole potatoes, is a gourmand for bacon, drills holes in packing cases, and is daunted by nothing short of tin. All the while he does not neglect to vituperate the chipmunks and sparrows that whisk off crumbs of comfort from under the camper's feet. The Camp Robber's gray coat, black and white barred wings, and slender bill, with certain tricks of perching, accuse him of attempts to pass himself off among woodpeckers; but his behavior is all crow. He frequents the higher pine belts, and has a noisy strident call like a jay's, and how clean he and the frisk-tailed chipmunks keep the camp! No crumb or paring or bit of eggshell goes amiss.

High as the camp may be, so it is not above timber-line, it is not too high for the coyote, the bobcat, or the wolf. It is the complaint of the ordinary camper that the woods are too still, depleted of wild life. But what dead body of wild thing, or neglected game untouched by its kind, do you find? And put out offal away from camp over night, and look next day at the foot tracks where it lay.

Man is a great blunderer going about in the woods, and there is no other except the bear makes so much noise. Being so well warned beforehand, it is a very stupid animal, or a very bold one, that cannot keep safely hid. The cunningest hunter is hunted in turn, and what he leaves of his kill is meat for some other. That is the economy of nature, but with it all there is not sufficient account taken of the works of man. There is no scavenger that eats tin cans, and no wild thing leaves a like disfigurement on the forest floor.

The Pocket Hunter

I remember very well when I first met him. Walking in the evening glow to spy the marriages of the white gilias, I sniffed the unmistakable odor of burning sage. It is a smell that carries far and indicates usually the nearness of a campoodie, but on the level mesa nothing taller showed than Diana's sage. Over the tops of it, beginning to dusk under a young white moon, trailed a wavering ghost of smoke, and at the end of it I came upon the Pocket Hunter making a dry camp in the friendly scrub. He sat tailorwise in the sand, with his coffee-pot on the coals, his supper ready to hand in the frying pan, and himself in a mood for talk. His pack burros in hobbles strayed off to hunt for a wetter mouthful than the sage afforded, and gave him no concern.

We came upon him often after that, threading the windy passes, or by waterholes in the desert hills, and got to know much of his way of life. He was a small, bowed man, with a face and manner and speech of no character at all, as if he had that faculty of small hunted things of taking on the protective color of his surroundings. His clothes were of no fashion that I could remember, except that they bore liberal markings of pot black, and he had a curious fashion of going about with his mouth open, which gave him a vacant look until you came near enough to perceive him busy about an endless hummed, wordless tune. He traveled far and took a long time to it, but the simplicity of his kitchen arrangements was elemental. A pot for beans, a coffee-pot, a frying-pan, a tin to mix bread in—he fed the burros in this when there was need—with these he had been half round our western world and back. He explained to me very early in our acquaintance what was good to take to the hills for

food: nothing sticky, for that "dirtied the pots;" nothing with
"juice" to it, for that would not pack to advantage; and nothing likely to ferment. He used no gun, but he would set snares by the water-
holes for quail and doves, and in the trout country he carried a line.
Burros he kept, one or two according to his pack, for this chief
excellence, that they would eat potato parings and firewood. He had
owned a horse in the foothill country, but when he came to the
desert with no forage but mesquite, he found himself under the
necessity of picking the beans from the briers, a labor that drove
him to the use of pack animals to whom thorns were a relish.

I suppose no man becomes a pocket hunter by first intention. He
must be born with the faculty, and along comes the occasion, like
the tap on the test tube that induces crystallization. My friend had
been several things of no moment until he struck a thousand-
dollar pocket in the Lee District and came into his vocation. A
pocket, you must know, is a small body of rich ore occurring by
itself, or in a vein of poorer stuff. Nearly every mineral ledge con-
tains such, if only one has the luck to hit upon them without too
much labor. The sensible thing for a man to do who has found a
good pocket is to buy himself into business and keep away from the
hills. The logical thing is to set out looking for another one. My
friend the Pocket Hunter had been looking twenty years. His working outfit was a shovel, a pick, a gold pan which he kept cleaner
than his plate, and a pocket magnifier. When he came to a watercourse he would pan out the gravel of its bed for "colors," and under
the glass determine if they had come from far or near, and so spy-
ing he would work up the stream until he found where the drift of
the gold-bearing outcrop fanned out into the creek; then up the
side of the cañon till he came to the proper vein. I think he said the
best indication of small pockets was an iron stain, but I could never
get the run of miner's talk enough to feel instructed for pocket
hunting. He had another method in the waterless hills, where he
would work in and out of blind gullies and all windings of the
manifold strata that appeared not to have cooled since they had
been heaved up. His itinerary began with the east slope of the
Sierras of the Snows, where that range swings across to meet the
coast hills, and all up that slope to the Truckee River country,

where the long cold forbade his progress north. Then he worked
back down one or another of the nearly parallel ranges that lie out
desertward, and so down to the sink of the Mojave River, burrowing
to oblivion in the sand,—a big mysterious land, a lonely, inhos-
pitable land, beautiful, terrible. But he came to no harm in it; the
land tolerated him as it might a gopher or a badger. Of all its inhabitants it has the least concern for man.

There are many strange sorts of humans bred in a mining country, each sort despising the queernesses of the other, but of them all
I found the Pocket Hunter most acceptable for his clean, compan-
ionable talk. There was more color to his reminiscences than the
faded sandy old miners "kyoteing," that is, tunneling like a coyote
(kyote in the vernacular) in the core of a lonesome hill. Such a one
has found, perhaps, a body of tolerable ore in a poor lead,—remember that I can never be depended on to get the terms right,—and
followed it into the heart of country rock to no profit, hoping, burrowing, and hoping. These men go harmlessly mad in time, believ-
ing themselves just behind the wall of fortune—most likable and
simple men, for whom it is well to do any kindly thing that occurs
to you except lend them money. I have known "grub stakers" too,
those persuasive sinners to whom you make allowances of flour and
pork and coffee in consideration of the ledges they are about to
find; but none of these proved so much worth while as the Pocket
Hunter. He wanted nothing of you and maintained a cheerful pref-
erence for his own way of life. It was an excellent way if you had the
constitution for it. The Pocket Hunter had gotten to that point
where he knew no bad weather, and all places were equally happy
so long as they were out of doors. I do not know just how long it
takes to become saturated with the elements so that one takes no
account of them. Myself can never get past the glow and exhilaration of a storm, the wrestle of long dust-heavy winds, the play of
live thunder on the rocks, nor past the keen fret of fatigue when the
storm outlasts physical endurance. But prospectors and Indians get
a kind of a weather shell that remains on the body until death.

The Pocket Hunter had seen destruction by the violence of
nature and the violence of men, and felt himself in the grip of an
All-wisdom that killed men or spared them as seemed for their

good; but of death by sickness he knew nothing except that he
believed he should never suffer it. He had been in Grape-vine
Cañon the year of storms that changed the whole front of the
mountain. All day he had come down under the wing of the storm,
hoping to win past it, but finding it traveling with him until night.
It kept on after that, he supposed, a steady downpour, but could not
with certainty say, being securely deep in sleep. But the weather
instinct does not sleep. In the night the heavens behind the hill dissolved in rain, and the roar of the storm was borne in and mixed
with his dreaming, so that it moved him, still asleep, to get up and
out of the path of it. What finally woke him was the crash of pine
logs as they went down before the unbridled flood, and the swirl of
foam that lashed him where he clung in the tangle of scrub while
the wall of water went by. It went on against the cabin of Bill Gerry
and laid Bill stripped and broken on a sand bar at the mouth of the
Grape-vine, seven miles away. There, when the sun was up and the
wrath of the rain spent, the Pocket Hunter found and buried him;
but he never laid his own escape at any door but the unintelligible
favor of the Powers.

The journeyings of the Pocket Hunter led him often into that
mysterious country beyond Hot Creek where a hidden force works
mischief, mole-like, under the crust of the earth. Whatever agency
is at work in that neighborhood, and it is popularly supposed to be
the devil, it changes means and direction without time or season. It
creeps up whole hillsides with insidious heat, unguessed until one
notes the pine woods dying at the top, and having scorched out a
good block of timber returns to steam and spout in caked, forgotten
crevices of years before. It will break up sometimes blue-hot and
bubbling, in the midst of a clear creek, or make a sucking, scalding
quicksand at the ford. These outbreaks had the kind of morbid
interest for the Pocket Hunter that a house of unsavory reputation
has in a respectable neighborhood, but I always found the accounts
he brought me more interesting than his explanations, which were
compounded of fag ends of miner's talk and superstition. He was a
perfect gossip of the woods, this Pocket Hunter, and when I could
get him away from "leads" and "strikes" and "contacts," full of
fascinating small talk about the ebb and flood of creeks, the piñon

crop on Black Mountain, and the wolves of Mesquite Valley. I suppose he never knew how much he depended for the necessary sense
of home and companionship on the beasts and trees, meeting and
finding them in their wonted places,—the bear that used to come
down Pine Creek in the spring, pawing out trout from the shelters
of sod banks, the juniper at Lone Tree Spring, and the quail at
Paddy Jack's.

There is a place on Waban, south of White Mountain, where flat,
wind-tilted cedars make low tents and coves of shade and shelter,
where the wild sheep winter in the snow. Woodcutters and prospectors had brought me word of that, but the Pocket Hunter was acces-
sory to the fact. About the opening of winter, when one looks for
sudden big storms, he had attempted a crossing by the nearest path,
beginning the ascent at noon. It grew cold, the snow came on thick
and blinding, and wiped out the trail in a white smudge; the storm
drift blew in and cut off landmarks, the early dark obscured the rising drifts. According to the Pocket Hunter's account, he knew where
he was, but couldn't exactly say. Three days before he had been in
the west arm of Death Valley on a short water allowance, ankle-
deep in shifty sand; now he was on the rise of Waban, knee-deep in
sodden snow, and in both cases he did the only allowable thing—
he walked on. That is the only thing to do in a snowstorm in any
case. It might have been the creature instinct, which in his way of
life had room to grow, that led him to the cedar shelter; at any rate
he found it about four hours after dark, and heard the heavy
breathing of the flock. He said that if he thought at all at this junc-
ture he must have thought that he had stumbled on a storm-belat-
ed shepherd with his silly sheep; but in fact he took no note of anything but the warmth of packed fleeces, and snuggled in between
them dead with sleep. If the flock stirred in the night he stirred
drowsily to keep close and let the storm go by. That was all until
morning woke him shining on a white world. Then the very soul of
him shook to see the wild sheep of God stand up about him, nodding their great horns beneath the cedar roof, looking out on the
wonder of the snow. They had moved a little away from him with
the coming of the light, but paid him no more heed. The light
broadened and the white pavilions of the snow swam in the

heavenly blueness of the sea from which they rose. The cloud drift scattered and broke billowing in the cañons. The leader stamped lightly on the litter to put the flock in motion, suddenly they took the drifts in those long light leaps that are nearest to flight, down and away on the slopes of Waban. Think of that to happen to a Pocket Hunter! But though he had fallen on many a wished-for hap, he was curiously inapt at getting the truth about beasts in general. He believed in the venom of toads, and charms for snake bites, and—for this I could never forgive him—had all the miner's prejudices against my friend the coyote. Thief, sneak, and son of a thief were the friendliest words he had for this little gray dog of the wilderness.

Of course with so much seeking he came occasionally upon pockets of more or less value, otherwise he could not have kept up his way of life; but he had as much luck in missing great ledges as in finding small ones. He had been all over the Tonopah country, and brought away float without happening upon anything that gave promise of what that district was to become in a few years. He claimed to have chipped bits off the very outcrop of the California Rand, without finding it worth while to bring away, but none of these things put him out of countenance.

It was once in roving weather, when we found him shifting pack on a steep trail, that I observed certain of his belongings done up in green canvas bags, the veritable "green bag" of English novels. It seemed so incongruous a reminder in this untenanted West that I dropped down beside the trail overlooking the vast dim valley, to hear about the green canvas. He had gotten it, he said, in London years before, and that was the first I had known of his having been abroad. It was after one of his "big strikes" that he had made the Grand Tour, and had brought nothing away from it but the green canvas bags, which he conceived would fit his needs, and an ambition. This last was nothing less than to strike it rich and set himself up among the eminently bourgeois of London. It seemed that the situation of the wealthy English middle class, with just enough gentility above to aspire to, and sufficient smaller fry to bully and patronize, appealed to his imagination, though of course he did not put it so crudely as that.

It was no news to me then, two or three years after, to learn that he had taken ten thousand dollars from an abandoned claim, just the sort of luck to have pleased him, and gone to London to spend it. The land seemed not to miss him any more than it had minded him, but I missed him and could not forget the trick of expecting him in least likely situations. Therefore it was with a pricking sense of the familiar that I followed a twilight trail of smoke, a year or two later, to the swale of a dripping spring, and came upon a man by the fire with a coffee-pot and frying-pan. I was not surprised to find it was the Pocket Hunter. No man can be stronger than his destiny.

Shoshone Land

It is true I have been in Shoshone Land, but before that, long before, I had seen it through the eyes of Winnenap' in a rosy mist of reminiscence, and must always see it with a sense of intimacy in the light that never was. Sitting on the golden slope at the campoodie, looking across the Bitter Lake to the purple tops of Mutarango, the medicine-man drew up its happy places one by one, like little blessed islands in a sea of talk. For he was born a Shoshone, was Winnenap'; and though his name, his wife, his children, and his tribal relations were of the Paiutes, his thoughts turned homesickly toward Shoshone Land. Once a Shoshone always a Shoshone. Winnenap' lived gingerly among the Paiutes and in his heart despised them. But he could speak a tolerable English when he would, and he always would if it were of Shoshone Land.

He had come into the keeping of the Paiutes as a hostage for the long peace which the authority of the whites made interminable, and, though there was now no order in the tribe, nor any power that could have lawfully restrained him, kept on in the old usage, to save his honor and the word of his vanished kin. He had seen his children's children in the borders of the Paiutes, but loved best his own miles of sand and rainbow-painted hills. Professedly he had not seen them since the beginning of his hostage; but every year about the end of the rains and before the strength of the sun had come upon us from the south, the medicine-man went apart on the mountains to gather herbs, and when he came again I knew by the new fortitude of his countenance and the new color of his reminiscences that he had been alone and unspied upon in Shoshone Land.

To reach that country from the campoodie, one goes south and south, within hearing of the lip-lip-lapping of the great tideless lake, and south by east over a high rolling district, miles and miles of sage and nothing else. So one comes to the country of the painted hills,—old red cones of craters, wasteful beds of mineral earths, hot, acrid springs, and steam jets issuing from a leprous soil. After the hills the black rock, after the craters the spewed lava, ash strewn, of incredible thickness, and full of sharp, winding rifts. There are picture writings carved deep in the face of the cliffs to mark the way for those who do not know it. On the very edge of the black rock the earth falls away in a wide sweeping hollow, which is Shoshone Land.

South the land rises in very blue hills, blue because thickly wooded with ceanothus and manzanita, the haunt of deer and the border of the Shoshones. Eastward the land goes very far by broken ranges, narrow valleys of pure desertness, and huge mesas uplifted to the sky-line, east and east, and no man knows the end of it.

It is the country of the bighorn, the wapiti, and the wolf, nesting place of buzzards, land of cloud-nourished trees and wild things that live without drink. Above all, it is the land of the creosote and the mesquite. The mesquite is God's best thought in all this desertness. It grows in the open, is thorny, stocky, close grown, and iron-rooted. Long winds move in the draughty valleys, blown sand fills and fills about the lower branches, piling pyramidal dunes, from the top of which the mesquite twigs flourish greenly. Fifteen or twenty feet under the drift, where it seems no rain could penetrate, the main trunk grows, attaining often a yard's thickness, resistant as oak. In Shoshone Land one digs for large timber; that is in the southerly, sandy exposures. Higher on the tabletopped ranges low trees of juniper and piñon stand each apart, rounded and spreading heaps of greenness. Between them, but each to itself in smooth clear spaces, tufts of tall feathered grass.

This is the sense of the desert hills, that there is room enough and time enough. Trees grow to consummate domes; every plant has its perfect work. Noxious weeds such as come up thickly in crowded fields do not flourish in the free spaces. Live long enough with an Indian, and he or the wild things will show you a use for everything that grows in these borders.

The manner of the country makes the usage of life there, and the land will not be lived in except in its own fashion. The Shoshones live like their trees, with great spaces between, and in pairs and in family groups they set up wattled huts by the infrequent springs. More wickiups than two make a very great number. Their shelters are lightly built, for they travel much and far, following where deer feed and seeds ripen, but they are not more lonely than other creatures that inhabit there.

The year's round is somewhat in this fashion. After the piñon harvest the clans foregather on a warm southward slope for the annual adjustment of tribal difficulties and the medicine dance, for marriage and mourning and vengeance, and the exchange of serviceable information; if, for example, the deer have shifted their feeding ground, if the wild sheep have come back to Waban, or certain springs run full or dry. Here the Shoshones winter flockwise, weaving baskets and hunting big game driven down from the country of the deep snow. And this brief intercourse is all the use they have of their kind, for now there are no wars, and many of their ancient crafts have fallen into disuse. The solitariness of the life breeds in the men, as in the plants, a certain well-roundedness and sufficiency to its own ends. Any Shoshone family has in itself the man-seed, power to multiply and replenish, potentialities for food and clothing and shelter, for healing and beautifying.

When the rain is over and gone they are stirred by the instinct of those that journeyed eastward from Eden, and go up each with his mate and young brood, like birds to old nesting places. The beginning of spring in Shoshone Land—oh the soft wonder of it!—is a mistiness as of incense smoke, a veil of greenness over the whitish stubby shrubs, a web of color on the silver sanded soil. No counting covers the multitude of rayed blossoms that break suddenly underfoot in the brief season of the winter rains, with silky furred or prickly viscid foliage, or no foliage at all. They are morning and evening bloomers chiefly, and strong seeders. Years of scant rains they lie shut and safe in the winnowed sands, so that some species appear to be extinct. Years of long storms they break so thickly into bloom that no horse treads without crushing them. These years the gullies of the hills are rank with fern and a great tangle of climbing vines.

Just as the mesa twilights have their vocal note in the love call of the burrowing owl, so the desert spring is voiced by the mourning doves. Welcome and sweet they sound in the smoky mornings before breeding time, and where they frequent in any great numbers water is confidently looked for. Still by the springs one finds the cunning brush shelters from which the Shoshones shot arrows at them when the doves came to drink.

Now as to these same Shoshones there are some who claim that they have no right to the name, which belongs to a more northerly tribe; but that is the word they will be called by, and there is no greater offense than to call an Indian out of his name. According to their traditions and all proper evidence, they were a great people occupying far north and east of their present bounds, driven thence by the Paiutes. Between the two tribes is the residuum of old hostilities.

Winnenap', whose memory ran to the time when the boundary of the Paiute country was a dead-line to Shoshones, told me once how himself and another lad, in an unforgotten spring, discovered a nesting place of buzzards a bit of a way beyond the borders. And they two burned to rob those nests. Oh, for no purpose at all except as boys rob nests immemorially, for the fun of it, to have and handle and show to other lads as an exceeding treasure, and afterwards discard. So, not quite meaning to, but breathless with daring, they crept up a gully, across a sage brush flat and through a waste of boulders, to the rugged pines where their sharp eyes had made out the buzzards settling.

The medicine-man told me, always with a quaking relish at this point, that while they, grown bold by success, were still in the tree, they sighted a Paiute hunting party crossing between them and their own land. That was mid-morning, and all day on into the dark the boys crept and crawled and slid, from boulder to bush, and bush to boulder, in cactus scrub and on naked sand, always in a sweat of fear, until the dust caked in the nostrils and the breath sobbed in the body, around and away many a mile until they came to their own land again. And all the time Winnenap' carried those buzzard's eggs in the slack of his single buckskin garment! Young Shoshones are like young quail, knowing without teaching about feeding and hiding, and learning what civilized children never learn, to be still and to keep on being still, at the first hint of danger or strangeness.

As for food, that appears to be chiefly a matter of being willing. Desert Indians all eat chuck-wallas, big black and white lizards that have delicate white flesh savored like chicken. Both the Shoshones and the coyotes are fond of the flesh of *Gopherus agassizii*, the turtle that by feeding on buds, going without drink, and burrowing in the sand through the winter, contrives to live a known period of twenty-five years. It seems that most seeds are foodful in the arid regions, most berries edible, and many shrubs good for firewood with the sap in them. The mesquite bean, whether the screw or straight pod, pounded to a meal, boiled to a kind of mush, and dried in cakes, sulphur-colored and needing an axe to cut it, is an excellent food for long journeys. Fermented in water with wild honey and the honeycomb, it makes a pleasant, mildly intoxicating drink.

Next to spring, the best time to visit Shoshone Land is when the deer-star hangs low and white like a torch over the morning hills. Go up past Winnedumah and down Saline and up again to the rim of Mesquite Valley. Take no tent, but if you will, have an Indian build you a wickiup, willows planted in a circle, drawn over to an arch, and bound cunningly with withes, all the leaves on, and chinks to count the stars through. But there was never any but Winnenap' who could tell and make it worth telling about Shoshone Land.

And Winnenap' will not any more. He died, as do most medicine-men of the Paiutes.

Where the lot falls when the campoodie chooses a medicine-man there it rests. It is an honor a man seldom seeks but must wear, an honor with a condition. When three patients die under his ministrations, the medicine-man must yield his life and his office. Wounds do not count; broken bones and bullet holes the Indian can understand, but measles, pneumonia, and smallpox are witchcraft. Winnenap' was medicine-man for fifteen years. Besides considerable skill in healing herbs, he used his prerogatives cunningly. It is permitted the medicine-man to decline the case when the patient has had treatment from any other, say the white doctor, whom many of the younger generation consult. Or, if before having seen the patient, he can definitely refer his disorder to some supernatural cause wholly out of the medicine-man's jurisdiction, say to the spite of an evil spirit going about in the form of a coyote, and states the case convincingly, he may avoid the penalty. But this must not be pushed too far. All else failing, he can hide. Winnenap' did this the time of the measles epidemic. Returning from his yearly herb gathering, he heard of it at Black Rock, and turning aside, he was not to be found, nor did he return to his own place until the disease had spent itself, and half the children of the campoodie were in their shallow graves with beads sprinkled over them.

It is possible the tale of Winnenap's patients had not been strictly kept. There had not been a medicine-man killed in the valley for twelve years, and for that the perpetrators had been severely punished by the whites. The winter of the Big Snow an epidemic of pneumonia carried off the Indians with scarcely a warning; from the lake northward to the lava flats they died in the sweat-houses, and under the hands of the medicine-men. Even the drugs of the white physician had no power.

After two weeks of this plague the Paiutes drew to council to consider the remissness of their medicine-men. They were sore with grief and afraid for themselves; as a result of the council, one in every campoodie was sentenced to the ancient penalty. But schooling and native shrewdness had raised up in the younger men an unfaith in old usages, so judgment halted between sentence and execution. At Three Pines the government teacher brought out influential whites to threaten and cajole the stubborn tribes. At Tunawai the conservatives sent into Nevada for that pacific old humbug, Johnson Sides, most notable of Paiute orators, to harangue his people. Citizens of the towns turned out with food and comforts, and so after a season the trouble passed.

But here at Maverick there was no school, no oratory, and no alleviation. One third of the campoodie died, and the rest killed the medicine-men. Winnenap' expected it, and for days walked and sat a little apart from his family that he might meet it as became a Shoshone, no doubt suffering the agony of dread deferred. When finally three men came and sat at his fire without greeting he knew his time. He turned a little from them, dropped his chin upon his knees, and looked out over Shoshone Land, breathing evenly. The women went into the wickiup and covered their heads with their blankets.

So much has the Indian lost of savageness by merely desisting from killing, that the executioners braved themselves to their work by drinking and a show of quarrelsomeness. In the end a sharp hatchet stroke discharged the duty of the campoodie. Afterward his women buried him, and a warm wind coming out of the south, the force of the disease was broken, and even they acquiesced in the wisdom of the tribe. That summer they told me all except the names of the Three.

Since it appears that we make our own heaven here, no doubt we shall have a hand in the heaven of hereafter; and I know what Winnenap's will be like: worth going to if one has leave to live in it according to his liking. It will be tawny gold underfoot, walled up with jacinth and jasper, ribbed with chalcedony, and yet no hymnbook heaven, but the free air and free spaces of Shoshone Land.

Jimville—A Bret Harte Town

When Mr. Harte found himself with a fresh palette and his particular local color fading from the West, he did what he considered the only safe thing, and carried his young impression away to be worked out untroubled by any newer fact. He should have gone to Jimville. There he would have found cast up on the ore-ribbed hills the bleached timbers of more tales, and better ones.

You could not think of Jimville as anything more than a survival, like the herb-eating, bony-cased old tortoise that pokes cheerfully about those borders some thousands of years beyond his proper epoch. Not that Jimville is old, but it has an atmosphere favorable to the type of a half century back, if not "forty-niners," of that breed. It is said of Jimville that getting away from it is such a piece of work that it encourages permanence in the population; the fact is that most have been drawn there by some real likeness or liking. Not however that I would deny the difficulty of getting into or out of that cove of reminder, I who have made the journey so many times at great pains of a poor body. Any way you go at it, Jimville is about three days from anywhere in particular. North or south, after the railroad there is a stage journey of such interminable monotony as induces forgetfulness of all previous states of existence.

The road to Jimville is the happy hunting ground of old stagecoaches bought up from superseded routes the West over, rocking, lumbering, wide vehicles far gone in the odor of romance, coaches that Vasquez has held up, from whose high seats express messengers have shot or been shot as their luck held. This is to comfort you when the driver stops to rummage for wire to mend a failing bolt.

There is enough of this sort of thing to quite prepare you to believe what the driver insists, namely, that all that country and Jimville are held together by wire.

First on the way to Jimville you cross a lonely open land, with a hint in the sky of things going on under the horizon, a palpitant, white, hot land where the wheels gird at the sand and the midday heaven shuts it in breathlessly like a tent. So in still weather; and when the wind blows there is occupation enough for the passengers, shifting seats to hold down the windward side of the wagging coach. This is a mere trifle. The Jimville stage is built for five passengers, but when you have seven, with four trunks, several parcels, three sacks of grain, the mail and express, you begin to understand that proverb about the road which has been reported to you. In time you learn to engage the high seat beside the driver, where you get good air and the best company. Beyond the desert rise the lava flats, scoriae strewn; sharp-cutting walls of narrow cañons; league-wide, frozen puddles of black rock, intolerable and forbidding. Beyond the lava the mouths that spewed it out, ragged-lipped, ruined craters shouldering to the cloud-line, mostly of red earth, as red as a red heifer. These have some comforting of shrubs and grass. You get the very spirit of the meaning of that country when you see Little Pete feeding his sheep in the red, choked maw of an old vent,—a kind of silly pastoral gentleness that glozes over an elemental violence. Beyond the craters rise worn, auriferous hills of a quiet sort, tumbled together; a valley full of mists; whitish green scrub; and bright, small, panting lizards; then Jimville.

The town looks to have spilled out of Squaw Gulch, and that, in fact, is the sequence of its growth. It began around the Bully Boy and Theresa group of mines midway up Squaw Gulch, spreading down to the smelter at the mouth of the ravine. The freight wagons dumped their loads as near to the mill as the slope allowed, and Jimville grew in between. Above the Gulch begins a pine wood with sparsely grown thickets of lilac, azalea, and odorous blossoming shrubs.

Squaw Gulch is a very sharp, steep, ragged-walled ravine, and that part of Jimville which is built in it has only one street,—in summer paved with bone-white cobbles, in the wet months a frothy yellow flood. All between the ore dumps and solitary small cabins, pieced out with tin cans and packing cases, run footpaths drawing down to the Silver Dollar saloon. When Jimville was having the time of its life the Silver Dollar had those same coins let into the bar top for a border, but the proprietor pried them out when the glory departed. There are three hundred inhabitants in Jimville and four bars, though you are not to argue anything from that.

Hear now how Jimville came by its name. Jim Calkins discovered the Bully Boy, Jim Baker located the Theresa. When Jim Jenkins opened an eating-house in his tent he chalked up on the flap, "Best meals in Jimville, $1.00," and the name stuck.

There was more human interest in the origin of Squaw Gulch, though it tickled no humor. It was Dimmick's squaw from Aurora way. If Dimmick had been anything except New Englander he would have called her a mahala, but that would not have bettered his behavior. Dimmick made a strike, went East, and the squaw who had been to him as his wife took to drink. That was the bald way of stating it in the Aurora country. The milk of human kindness, like some wine, must not be uncorked too much in speech lest it lose savor. This is what they did. The woman would have returned to her own people, being far gone with child, but the drink worked her bane. By the river of this ravine her pains overtook her. There Jim Calkins, prospecting, found her dying with a three days' babe nozzling at her breast. Jim heartened her for the end, buried her, and walked back to Poso, eighteen miles, the child poking in the folds of his denim shirt with small mewing noises, and won support for it from the rough-handed folks of that place. Then he came back to Squaw Gulch, so named from that day, and discovered the Bully Boy. Jim humbly regarded this piece of luck as interposed for his reward, and I for one believed him. If it had been in mediaeval times you would have had a legend or a ballad. Bret Harte would have given you a tale. You see in me a mere recorder, for I know what is best for you; you shall blow out this bubble from your own breath.

You could never get into any proper relation to Jimville unless you could slough off and swallow your acquired prejudices as a lizard does his skin. Once wanting some womanly attentions, the stage-driver assured me I might have them at the Nine-Mile House from the lady barkeeper. The phrase tickled all my after-dinner coffee sense of humor into an anticipation of Poker Flat. The stage-driver proved himself really right, though you are not to suppose from this that Jimville had no conventions and no caste. They work out these things in the personal equation largely. Almost every latitude of behavior is allowed a good fellow, one no liar, a free spender, and a backer of his friends' quarrels. You are respected in as much ground as you can shoot over, in as many pretensions as you can make good.

That probably explains Mr. Fanshawe, the gentlemanly faro dealer of those parts, built for the rôle of Oakhurst, going white-shirted and frock-coated in a community of overalls; and persuading you that whatever shifts and tricks of the game were laid to his deal, he could not practice them on a person of your penetration. But he does. By his own account and the evidence of his manners he had been bred for a clergyman, and he certainly has gifts for the part. You find him always in possession of your point of view, and with an evident though not obtrusive desire to stand well with you. For an account of his killings, for his way with women and the way of women with him, I refer you to Brown of Calaveras and some others of that stripe. His improprieties had a certain sanction of long standing not accorded to the gay ladies who wore Mr. Fanshawe's favors. There were perhaps too many of them. On the whole, the point of the moral distinctions of Jimville appears to be a point of honor, with an absence of humorous appreciation that strangers mistake for dullness. At Jimville they see behavior as history and judge it by facts, untroubled by invention and the dramatic sense. You glimpse a crude equity in their dealings with Wilkins, who had shot a man at Lone Tree, fairly, in an open quarrel. Rumor of it reached Jimville before Wilkins rested there in flight. I saw Wilkins, all Jimville saw him; in fact, he came into the Silver Dollar when we were holding a church fair and bought a pink silk pincushion. I have often wondered what became of it. Some of us shook hands with him, not because we did not know, but because we had not been officially notified, and there were those present who knew how it was themselves. When the sheriff arrived Wilkins had moved on, and Jimville organized a posse and brought him back, because the sheriff was a Jimville man and we had to stand by him.

I said we had the church fair at the Silver Dollar. We had most things there, dances, town meetings, and the kinetoscope exhibition of the Passion Play. The Silver Dollar had been built when the borders of Jimville spread from Minton to the red hill the Defiance twisted through. "Side-Winder" Smith scrubbed the floor for us and moved the bar to the back room. The fair was designed for the support of the circuit rider who preached to the few that would hear, and buried us all in turn. He was the symbol of Jimville's respectability, although he was of a sect that held dancing among the cardinal sins. The management took no chances on offending the minister; at 11.30 they tendered him the receipts of the evening in the chairman's hat, as a delicate intimation that the fair was closed. The company filed out of the front door and around to the back. Then the dance began formally with no feelings hurt. These were the sort of courtesies, common enough in Jimville, that brought tears of delicate inner laughter.

There were others besides Mr. Fanshawe who had walked out of Mr. Harte's demesne to Jimville and wore names that smacked of the soil,—"Alkali Bill," "Pike" Wilson, "Three Finger," and "Mono Jim;" fierce, shy, profane, sun-dried derelicts of the windy hills, who each owned, or had owned, a mine and was wishful to own one again. They laid up on the worn benches of the Silver Dollar or the Same Old Luck like beached vessels, and their talk ran on endlessly of "strike" and "contact" and "mother lode," and worked around to fights and hold-ups, villainy, haunts, and the hoodoo of the Minietta, told austerely without imagination.

Do not suppose I am going to repeat it all; you who want these things written up from the point of view of people who do not do them every day would get no savor in their speech.

Says Three Finger, relating the history of the Mariposa, "I took it off'n Tom Beatty, cheap, after his brother Bill was shot."

Says Jim Jenkins, "What was the matter of him?"

"Who? Bill? Abe Johnson shot him; he was fooling around Johnson's wife, an' Tom sold me the mine dirt cheap."

"Why didn't he work it himself?"

"Him? Oh, he was laying for Abe and calculated to have to leave the country pretty quick."

"Huh!" says Jim Jenkins, and the tale flows smoothly on.

Yearly the spring fret floats the loose population of Jimville out into the desolate waste hot lands, guiding by the peaks and a few rarely touched water-holes, always, always with the golden hope. They develop prospects and grow rich, develop others and grow poor but never embittered. Say the hills, It is all one, there is gold enough, time enough, and men enough to come after you. And at Jimville they understand the language of the hills.

Jimville does not know a great deal about the crust of the earth, it prefers a "hunch." That is an intimation from the gods that if you go over a brown back of the hills, by a dripping spring, up Coso way, you will find what is worth while. I have never heard that the failure of any particular hunch disproved the principle. Somehow the rawness of the land favors the sense of personal relation to the supernatural. There is not much intervention of crops, cities, clothes, and manners between you and the organizing forces to cut off communication. All this begets in Jimville a state that passes explanation unless you will accept an explanation that passes belief. Along with killing and drunkenness, coveting of women, charity, simplicity, there is a certain indifference, blankness, emptiness if you will, of all vaporings, no bubbling of the pot,—it wants the German to coin a word for that,—no bread-envy, no brother-fervor. Western writers have not sensed it yet; they smack the savor of lawlessness too much upon their tongues, but you have these to witness it is not mean-spiritedness. It is pure Greek in that it represents the courage to sheer off what is not worth while. Beyond that it endures without sniveling, renounces without self-pity, fears no death, rates itself not too great in the scheme of things; so do beasts, so did St. Jerome in the desert, so also in the elder day did gods. Life, its performance, cessation, is no new thing to gape and wonder at.

Here you have the repose of the perfectly accepted instinct which includes passion and death in its perquisites. I suppose that the end of all our hammering and yawping will be something like the point of view of Jimville. The only difference will be in the decorations.

My Neighbor's Field

It is one of those places God must have meant for a field from all time, lying very level at the foot of the slope that crowds up against Kearsarge, falling slightly toward the town. North and south it is fenced by low old glacial ridges, boulder strewn and untenable. Eastward it butts on orchard closes and the village gardens, brimming over into them by wild brier and creeping grass. The village street, with its double row of unlike houses, breaks off abruptly at the edge of the field in a footpath that goes up the streamside, beyond it, to the source of waters.

The field is not greatly esteemed of the town, not being put to the plough nor affording firewood, but breeding all manner of wild seeds that go down in the irrigating ditches to come up as weeds in the gardens and grass plots. But when I had no more than seen it in the charm of its spring smiling, I knew I should have no peace until I had bought ground and built me a house beside it, with a little wicket to go in and out at all hours, as afterward came about.

Edswick, Roeder, Connor, and Ruffin owned the field before it fell to my neighbor. But before that the Paiutes, mesne lords of the soil, made a campoodie by the rill of Pine Creek; and after, contesting the soil with them, cattle-men, who found its foodful pastures greatly to their advantage; and bands of blethering flocks shepherded by wild, hairy men of little speech, who attested their rights to the feeding ground with their long staves upon each other's skulls. Edswick homesteaded the field about the time the wild tide of mining life was roaring and rioting up Kearsarge, and where the village now stands built a stone hut, with loopholes to make good his claim against cattle-men or Indians. But Edswick died and

Roeder became master of the field. Roeder owned cattle on a thousand hills, and made it a recruiting ground for his bellowing herds before beginning the long drive to market across a shifty desert. He kept the field fifteen years, and afterward falling into difficulties, put it out as security against certain sums. Connor, who held the securities, was cleverer than Roeder and not so busy. The money fell due the winter of the Big Snow, when all the trails were forty feet under drifts, and Roeder was away in San Francisco selling his cattle. At the set time Connor took the law by the forelock and was adjudged possession of the field. Eighteen days later Roeder arrived on snowshoes, both feet frozen, and the money in his pack. In the long suit at law ensuing, the field fell to Ruffin, that clever one-armed lawyer with the tongue to wile a bird out of the bush, Connor's counsel, and was sold by him to my neighbor, whom from envying his possession I call Naboth.

Curiously, all this human occupancy of greed and mischief left no mark on the field, but the Indians did, and the unthinking sheep. Round its corners children pick up chipped arrow points of obsidian, scattered through it are kitchen middens and pits of old sweat-houses. By the south corner, where the campoodie stood, is a single shrub of "hoopee" (*Lycium Andersonii*), maintaining itself hardly among alien shrubs, and near by, three low rakish trees of hackberry, so far from home that no prying of mine has been able to find another in any cañon east or west. But the berries of both were food for the Paiutes, eagerly sought and traded for as far south as Shoshone Land. By the fork of the creek where the shepherds camp is a single clump of mesquite of the variety called "screw bean." The seed must have shaken there from some sheep's coat, for this is not the habitat of mesquite, and except for other single shrubs at sheep camps, none grows freely for a hundred and fifty miles south or east.

Naboth has put a fence about the best of the field, but neither the Indians nor the shepherds can quite forego it. They make camp and build their wattled huts about the borders of it, and no doubt they have some sense of home in its familiar aspect.

As I have said, it is a low-lying field, between the mesa and the town, with no hillocks in it, but a gentle swale where the waste water of the creek goes down to certain farms, and the hackberry-trees, of which the tallest might be three times the height of a man, are the tallest things in it. A mile up from the water gate that turns the creek into supply pipes for the town, begins a row of long-leaved pines, threading the watercourse to the foot of Kearsarge. These are the pines that puzzle the local botanist, not easily determined, and unrelated to other conifers of the Sierra slope; the same pines of which the Indians relate a legend mixed of brotherliness and the retribution of God. Once the pines possessed the field, as the worn stumps of them along the streamside show, and it would seem their secret purpose to regain their old footing. Now and then some seedling escapes the devastating sheep a rod or two down-stream. Since I came to live by the field one of these has tiptoed above the gully of the creek, beckoning the procession from the hills, as if in fact they would make back toward that skyward-pointing finger of granite on the opposite range, from which, according to the legend, when they were bad Indians and it a great chief, they ran away. This year the summer floods brought the round, brown, fruitful cones to my very door, and I look, if I live long enough, to see them come up greenly in my neighbor's field.

It is interesting to watch this retaking of old ground by the wild plants, banished by human use. Since Naboth drew his fence about the field and restricted it to a few wild-eyed steers, halting between the hills and the shambles, many old habitués of the field have come back to their haunts. The willow and brown birch, long ago cut off by the Indians for wattles, have come back to the streamside, slender and virginal in their spring greenness, and leaving long stretches of the brown water open to the sky. In stony places where no grass grows, wild olives sprawl; close-twigged, blue-gray patches in winter, more translucent greenish gold in spring than any aureole. Along with willow and birch and brier, the clematis, that shyest plant of water borders, slips down season by season to within a hundred yards of the village street. Convinced after three years that it would come no nearer, we spent time fruitlessly pulling up roots to plant in the garden. All this while, when no coaxing or care prevailed upon any transplanted slip to grow, one was coming up silently outside the fence near the wicket, coiling so secretly in the rabbit-brush that its presence was never suspected until it flowered delicately along its twining length. The horehound comes through the fence and under it, shouldering the pickets off the railings; the brier rose mines under the horehound; and no care, though I own I am not a close weeder, keeps the small pale moons of the primrose from rising to the night moth under my apple-trees. The first summer in the new place, a clump of cypripediums came up by the irrigating ditch at the bottom of the lawn. But the clematis will not come inside, nor the wild almond.

I have forgotten to find out, though I meant to, whether the wild almond grew in that country where Moses kept the flocks of his father-in-law, but if so one can account for the burning bush. It comes upon one with a flame-burst as of revelation; little hard red buds on leafless twigs, swelling unnoticeably, then one, two, or three strong suns, and from tip to tip one soft fiery glow, whispering with bees as a singing flame. A twig of finger size will be furred to the thickness of one's wrist by pink five-petaled bloom, so close that only the blunt-faced wild bees find their way in it. In this latitude late frosts cut off the hope of fruit too often for the wild almond to multiply greatly, but the spiny, tap-rooted shrubs are resistant to most plant evils.

It is not easy always to be attentive to the maturing of wild fruit. Plants are so unobtrusive in their material processes, and always at the significant moment some other bloom has reached its perfect hour. One can never fix the precise moment when the rosy tint the field has from the wild almond passes into the inspiring blue of lupines. One notices here and there a spike of bloom, and a day later the whole field royal and ruffling lightly to the wind. Part of the charm of the lupine is the continual stir of its plumes to airs not suspected otherwise. Go and stand by any crown of bloom and the tall stalks do but rock a little as for drowsiness, but look off across the field, and on the stillest days there is always a trepidation in the purple patches.

From midsummer until frost the prevailing note of the field is clear gold, passing into the rusty tone of bigelovia going into a decline, a succession of color schemes more admirably managed than the transformation scene at the theatre. Under my window a

colony of cleome made a soft web of bloom that drew me every
morning for a long still time; and one day I discovered that I was
looking into a rare fretwork of fawn and straw colored twigs from
which both bloom and leaf had gone, and I could not say if it had
been for a matter of weeks or days. The time to plant cucumbers
and set out cabbages may be set down in the almanac, but never
seed-time nor blossom in Naboth's field.

Certain winged and mailed denizens of the field seem to reach
their heyday along with the plants they most affect. In June the
leaning towers of the white milkweed are jeweled over with red and
gold beetles, climbing dizzily. This is that milkweed from whose
stems the Indians flayed fibre to make snares for small game, but
what use the beetles put it to except for a displaying ground for
their gay coats, I could never discover. The white butterfly crop
comes on with the bigelovia bloom, and on warm mornings makes
an airy twinkling all across the field. In September young linnets
grow out of the rabbit-brush in the night. All the nests discoverable in the neighboring orchards will not account for the numbers of them. Somewhere, by the same secret process by which the
field matures a million more seeds than it needs, it is maturing
red-hooded linnets for their devouring. All the purlieus of
bigelovia and artemisia are noisy with them for a month.
Suddenly as they come as suddenly go the fly-by-nights, that
pitch and toss on dusky barred wings above the field of summer
twilights. Never one of these nighthawks will you see after linnet
time, though the hurtle of their wings makes a pleasant sound
across the dusk in their season.

For two summers a great red-tailed hawk has visited the field
every afternoon between three and four o'clock, swooping and soar-
ing with the airs of a gentleman adventurer. What he finds there is
chiefly conjectured, so secretive are the little people of Naboth's
field. Only when leaves fall and the light is low and slant, one sees
the long clean flanks of the jackrabbits, leaping like small deer, and
of late afternoons little cotton-tails scamper in the runways. But the
most one sees of the burrowers, gophers, and mice is the fresh earth-
work of their newly opened doors, or the pitiful small shreds the
butcher-bird hangs on spiny shrubs.

It is a still field, this of my neighbor's, though so busy, and admirably compounded for variety and pleasantness,—a little sand, a little loam, a grassy plot, a stony rise or two, a full brown stream, a little touch of humanness, a footpath trodden out by moccasins. Naboth expects to make town lots of it and his fortune in one and the same day; but when I take the trail to talk with old Seyavi at the campoodie, it occurs to me that though the field may serve a good turn in those days it will hardly be happier. No, certainly not happier.

The Mesa Trail

The mesa trail begins in the campoodie at the corner of Naboth's field, though one may drop into it from the wood road toward the cañon, or from any of the cattle paths that go up along the stream-side; a clean, pale, smooth-trodden way between spiny shrubs, comfortably wide for a horse or an Indian. It begins, I say, at the campoodie, and goes on toward the twilight hills and the borders of Shoshone Land. It strikes diagonally across the foot of the hill-slope from the field until it reaches the larkspur level, and holds south along the front of Oppapago, having the high ranges to the right and the foothills and the great Bitter Lake below it on the left. The mesa holds very level here, cut across at intervals by the deep washes of dwindling streams, and its treeless spaces uncramp the soul.

Mesa trails were meant to be traveled on horseback, at the jigging coyote trot that only western-bred horses learn successfully. A foot-pace carries one too slowly past the units in a decorative scheme that is on a scale with the country round for bigness. It takes days' journeys to give a note of variety to the country of the social shrubs. These chiefly clothe the benches and eastern foot-slopes of the Sierras,—great spreads of artemisia, *coleogyne*, and spinosa, suffering no other woody stemmed thing in their purlieus; this by election apparently, with no elbowing; and the several shrubs have each their clientele of flowering herbs. It would be worth knowing how much the devastating sheep have had to do with driving the tender plants to the shelter of the prickle-bushes. It might have begun earlier, in the time Seyavi of the campoodie tells of, when antelope ran on the mesa like sheep for numbers, but scarcely any foot-high herb rears itself except from the midst of some stout twigged shrub; larkspur in the *coleogyne*, and for every spinosa the purpling coils of phacelia. In the shrub shelter, in the season, flock the little stemless things whose blossom time is as short as a marriage song. The larkspurs make the best showing, being tall and sweet, swaying a little above the shrubbery, scattering pollen dust which Navajo brides gather to fill their marriage baskets. This were an easier task than to find two of them of a shade. Larkspurs in the botany are blue, but if you were to slip rein to the stub of some black sage and set about proving it you would be still at it by the hour when the white gilias set their pale disks to the westering sun. This is the gilia the children call "evening snow," and it is no use trying to improve on children's names for wild flowers.

From the height of a horse you look down to clean spaces in a shifty yellow soil, bare to the eye as a newly sanded floor. Then as soon as ever the hill shadows begin to swell out from the sidelong ranges, come little flakes of whiteness fluttering at the edge of the sand. By dusk there are tiny drifts in the lee of every strong shrub, rosy-tipped corollas as riotous in the sliding mesa wind as if they were real flakes shaken out of a cloud, not sprung from the ground on wiry three-inch stems. They keep awake all night, and all the air is heavy and musky sweet because of them.

Farther south on the trail there will be poppies meeting ankle deep, and singly, peacock-painted bubbles of calochortus blown out at the tops of tall stems. But before the season is in tune for the gayer blossoms the best display of color is in the lupin wash. There is always a lupin wash somewhere on a mesa trail,—a broad, shallow, cobble-paved sink of vanished waters, where the hummocks of *Lupinus ornatus* run a delicate gamut from silvery green of spring to silvery white of winter foliage. They look in fullest leaf, except for color, most like the huddled huts of the campoodie, and the largest of them might be a man's length in diameter. In their season, which is after the gilias are at their best, and before the larkspurs are ripe for pollen gathering, every terminal whorl of the lupin sends up its blossom stalk, not holding any constant blue, but paling and purpling to guide the friendly bee to virginal honey sips, or away from the perfected and depleted flower. The length of the blossom stalk conforms to the rounded contour of the plant, and of these there will be a million moving indescribably in the airy current that flows down the swale of the wash.

There is always a little wind on the mesa, a sliding current of cooler air going down the face of the mountain of its own momentum, but not to disturb the silence of great space. Passing the wide mouths of cañons, one gets the effect of whatever is doing in them, openly or behind a screen of cloud,—thunder of falls, wind in the pine leaves, or rush and roar of rain. The rumor of tumult grows and dies in passing, as from open doors gaping on a village street, but does not impinge on the effect of solitariness. In quiet weather mesa days have no parallel for stillness, but the night silence breaks into certain mellow or poignant notes. Late afternoons the burrowing owls may be seen blinking at the doors of their hummocks with perhaps four or five elfish nestlings arow, and by twilight begin a soft *whoo-oo-ing*, rounder, sweeter, more incessant in mating time. It is not possible to disassociate the call of the burrowing owl from the late slant light of the mesa. If the fine vibrations which are the golden-violet glow of spring twilights were to tremble into sound, it would be just that mellow double note breaking along the blossom-tops. While the glow holds one sees the thistle-down flights and pouncings after prey, and on into the dark hears their soft *pus-ssh!* clearing out of the trail ahead. Maybe the pin-point shriek of field mouse or kangaroo rat that pricks the wakeful pauses of the night is extorted by these mellow-voiced plunderers, though it is just as like to be the work of the red fox on his twenty-mile constitutional.

Both the red fox and the coyote are free of the night hours, and both killers for the pure love of slaughter. The fox is no great talker, but the coyote goes garrulously through the dark in twenty keys at once, gossip, warning, and abuse. They are light treaders, the split-feet, so that the solitary camper sees their eyes about him in the dark sometimes, and hears the soft intake of breath when no leaf has stirred and no twig snapped underfoot. The coyote is your real lord of the mesa, and so he makes sure you are armed with no long black instrument to spit your teeth into his vitals at a thousand yards, is both bold and curious. Not so bold, however, as the badger and not so much of a curmudgeon. This short-legged meat-eater loves half lights and lowering days, has no friends, no enemies, and disowns his offspring. Very likely if he knew how hawk and crow dog him for dinners, he would resent it. But the badger is not very well contrived for looking up or far to either side. Dull afternoons he may be met nosing a trail hot-foot to the home of ground rat or squirrel, and is with difficulty persuaded to give the right of way. The badger is a pot-hunter and no sportsman. Once at the hill, he dives for the central chamber, his sharp-clawed, splayey feet splashing up the sand like a bather in the surf. He is a swift trailer, but not so swift or secretive but some small sailing hawk or lazy crow, perhaps one or two of each, has spied upon him and come drifting down the wind to the killing.

No burrower is so unwise as not to have several exits from his dwelling under protecting shrubs. When the badger goes down, as many of the furry people as are not caught napping come up by the back doors, and the hawks make short work of them. I suspect that the crows get nothing but the gratification of curiosity and the pickings of some secret store of seeds unearthed by the badger. Once the excavation begins they walk about expectantly, but the little gray hawks beat slow circles about the doors of exit, and are wiser in their generation, though they do not look it.

There are always solitary hawks sailing above the mesa, and where some blue tower of silence lifts out of the neighboring range, an eagle hanging dizzily, and always buzzards high up in the thin, translucent air making a merry-go-round. Between the coyote and the birds of carrion the mesa is kept clear of miserable dead.

The wind, too, is a besom over the treeless spaces, whisking new sand over the litter of the scant-leaved shrubs, and the little doorways of the burrowers are as trim as city fronts. It takes man to leave unsightly scars on the face of the earth. Here on the mesa the abandoned campoodies of the Paiutes are spots of desolation long after the wattles of the huts have warped in the brush heaps. The campoodies are near the watercourses, but never in the swale of the stream. The Paiute seeks rising ground, depending on air and sun for purification of his dwelling, and when it becomes wholly untenable, moves.

A campoodie at noontime, when there is no smoke rising and no stir of life, resembles nothing so much as a collection of prodigious wasps' nests. The huts are squat and brown and chimneyless, facing east, and the inhabitants have the faculty of quail for making themselves scarce in the underbrush at the approach of strangers. But they are really not often at home during midday, only the blind and incompetent left to keep the camp. These are working hours, and all across the mesa one sees the women whisking seeds of *chia* into their spoon-shaped baskets, these emptied again into the huge conical carriers, supported on the shoulders by a leather band about the forehead.

Mornings and late afternoons one meets the men singly and afoot on unguessable errands, or riding shaggy, browbeaten ponies, with game slung across the saddle-bows. This might be deer or even antelope, rabbits, or, very far south towards Shoshone Land, lizards.

There are myriads of lizards on the mesa, little gray darts, or larger salmon-sided ones that may be found swallowing their skins in the safety of a prickle-bush in early spring. Now and then a palm's breadth of the trail gathers itself together and scurries off with a little rustle under the brush, to resolve itself into sand again. This is pure witchcraft. If you succeed in catching it in transit, it loses its power and becomes a flat, horned, toad-like creature, horrid looking and harmless, of the color of the soil; and the curio dealer will give you two bits for it, to stuff.

Men have their season on the mesa as much as plants and four-footed things, and one is not like to meet them out of their time. For example, at the time of *rodeos*, which is perhaps April, one meets free riding vaqueros who need no trails and can find cattle where to the layman no cattle exist. As early as February bands of sheep work up from the south to the high Sierra pastures. It appears that shepherds have not changed more than sheep in the process of time. The shy hairy men who herd the tractile flocks might be, except for some added clothing, the very brethren of David. Of necessity they are hardy, simple livers, superstitious, fearful, given to seeing visions, and almost without speech. It needs the bustle of shearings and copious libations of sour, weak wine to restore the human faculty. Petite Pete, who works a circuit up from the Ceriso to Red Butte and around by way of Salt Flats, passes year by year on the mesa trail, his thick hairy chest thrown open to all weathers, twirling his long staff, and dealing brotherly with his dogs, who are possibly as intelligent, certainly handsomer.

A flock's journey is seven miles, ten if pasture fails, in a windless blur of dust, feeding as it goes, and resting at noons. Such hours Pete weaves a little screen of twigs between his head and the sun—the rest of him is as impervious as one of his own sheep—and sleeps while his dogs have the flocks upon their consciences. At night, wherever he may be, there Pete camps, and fortunate the trail-weary traveler who falls in with him. When the fire kindles and savory meat seethes in the pot, when there is a drowsy blether from the flock, and far down the mesa the twilight twinkle of shepherd fires, when there is a hint of blossom underfoot and a heavenly whiteness on the hills, one harks back without effort to Judaea and the Nativity. But one feels by day anything but good will to note the shorn shrubs and cropped blossom-tops. So many seasons' effort, so many suns and rains to make a pound of wool! And then there is the loss of ground-inhabiting birds that must fail from the mesa when few herbs ripen seed.

Out West, the west of the mesas and the unpatented hills, there is more sky than any place in the world. It does not sit flatly on the rim of earth, but begins somewhere out in the space in which the earth is poised, hollows more, and is full of clean winey winds. There are some odors, too, that get into the blood. There is the spring smell of sage that is the warning that sap is beginning to work in a soil that looks to have none of the juices of life in it; it is the sort of smell that sets one thinking what a long furrow the plough would turn up here, the sort of smell that is the beginning of new leafage, is best at the plant's best, and leaves a pungent trail where wild cattle crop. There is the smell of sage at sundown, burning sage from campoodies and sheep camps, that travels on the thin blue wraiths of smoke; the kind of smell that gets into the hair and garments, is not much liked except upon long acquaintance, and every Paiute and shepherd smells of it indubitably. There is the palpable smell of the bitter dust that comes up from the alkali flats at the end of the dry seasons, and the smell of rain from the wide-mouthed cañons. And last the smell of the salt grass country, which is the beginning of other things that are the end of the mesa trail.

The Basket Maker

"A man," says Seyavi of the campoodie, "must have a woman, but a woman who has a child will do very well."

That was perhaps why, when she lost her mate in the dying struggle of his race, she never took another, but set her wit to fend for herself and her young son. No doubt she was often put to it in the beginning to find food for them both. The Paiutes had made their last stand at the border of the Bitter Lake; battle-driven they died in its waters, and the land filled with cattle-men and adventurers for gold: this while Seyavi and the boy lay up in the caverns of the Black Rock and ate tule roots and fresh-water clams that they dug out of the slough bottoms with their toes. In the interim, while the tribes swallowed their defeat, and before the rumor of war died out, they must have come very near to the bare core of things. That was the time Seyavi learned the sufficiency of mother wit, and how much more easily one can do without a man than might at first be supposed.

To understand the fashion of any life, one must know the land it is lived in and the procession of the year. This valley is a narrow one, a mere trough between hills, a draught for storms, hardly a crow's flight from the sharp Sierras of the Snows to the curled, red and ochre, uncomforted, bare ribs of Waban. Midway of the groove runs a burrowing, dull river, nearly a hundred miles from where it cuts the lava flats of the north to its widening in a thick, tideless pool of a lake. Hereabouts the ranges have no foothills, but rise up steeply from the bench lands above the river. Down from the Sierras, for the east ranges have almost no rain, pour glancing white floods toward the lowest land, and all beside them lie the campoodies, brown wattled brush heaps, looking east.

In the river are mussels, and reeds that have edible white roots, and in the soddy meadows tubers of joint grass; all these at their best in the spring. On the slope the summer growth affords seeds; up the steep the one-leafed pines, an oily nut. That was really all they could depend upon, and that only at the mercy of the little gods of frost and rain. For the rest it was cunning against cunning, caution against skill, against quacking hordes of wild-fowl in the tulares, against pronghorn and bighorn and deer. You can guess, however, that all this warring of rifles and bowstrings, this influx of overlording whites, had made game wilder and hunters fearful of being hunted. You can surmise also, for it was a crude time and the land was raw, that the women became in turn the game of the conquerors.

There used to be in the Little Antelope a she dog, stray or outcast, that had a litter in some forsaken lair, and ranged and foraged for them, slinking savage and afraid, remembering and mistrusting humankind, wistful, lean, and sufficient for her young. I have thought Seyavi might have had days like that, and have had perfect leave to think, since she will not talk of it. Paiutes have the art of reducing life to its lowest ebb and yet saving it alive on grasshoppers, lizards, and strange herbs; and that time must have left no shift untried. It lasted long enough for Seyavi to have evolved the philosophy of life which I have set down at the beginning. She had gone beyond learning to do for her son, and learned to believe it worth while.

In our kind of society, when a woman ceases to alter the fashion of her hair, you guess that she has passed the crisis of her experience. If she goes on crimping and uncrimping with the changing mode, it is safe to suppose she has never come up against anything too big for her. The Indian woman gets nearly the same personal note in the pattern of her baskets. Not that she does not make all kinds, carriers, water-bottles, and cradles,—these are kitchen ware,—but her works of art are all of the same piece. Seyavi made flaring, flat-bottomed bowls, cooking pots really, when cooking was done by dropping hot stones into water-tight food baskets, and for decoration a design in colored bark of the procession of plumed crests of the valley quail. In this pattern she had made cooking pots in the golden spring of her wedding year, when the quail went up two and two to their resting places about the foot of Oppapago. In this fashion she made them when, after pillage, it was possible to reinstate the housewifely crafts. Quail ran then in the Black Rock by hundreds,—so you will still find them in fortunate years,—and in the famine time the women cut their long hair to make snares when the flocks came morning and evening to the springs.

Seyavi made baskets for love and sold them for money, in a generation that preferred iron pots for utility. Every Indian woman is an artist,—sees, feels, creates, but does not philosophize about her processes. Seyavi's bowls are wonders of technical precision, inside and out, the palm finds no fault with them, but the subtlest appeal is in the sense that warns us of humanness in the way the design spreads into the flare of the bowl. There used to be an Indian woman at Olancha who made bottle-neck trinket baskets in the rattlesnake pattern, and could accommodate the design to the swelling bowl and flat shoulder of the basket without sensible disproportion, and so cleverly that you might own one a year without thinking how it was done; but Seyavi's baskets had a touch beyond cleverness. The weaver and the warp lived next to the earth and were saturated with the same elements. Twice a year, in the time of white butterflies and again when young quail ran neck and neck in the chaparral, Seyavi cut willows for basketry by the creek where it wound toward the river against the sun and sucking winds. It never quite reached the river except in far-between times of summer flood, but it always tried, and the willows encouraged it as much as they could. You nearly always found them a little farther down than the trickle of eager water. The Paiute fashion of counting time appeals to me more than any other calendar. They have no stamp of heathen gods nor great ones, nor any succession of moons as have red men of the East and North, but count forward and back by the progress of the season; the time of *taboose*, before the trout begin to leap, the end of the piñon harvest, about the beginning of deep snows. So they get nearer the sense of the season, which runs early or late according as the rains are forward or delayed. But whenever Seyavi cut willows for baskets was always a golden time, and the soul of the weather went into the wood. If you had ever owned one of Seyavi's golden russet cooking bowls with the pattern of plumed quail, you would understand all this without saying anything.

Before Seyavi made baskets for the satisfaction of desire,—for that is a house-bred theory of art that makes anything more of it,—she danced and dressed her hair. In those days, when the spring was at flood and the blood pricked to the mating fever, the maids chose their flowers, wreathed themselves, and danced in the twilights, young desire crying out to young desire. They sang what the heart prompted, what the flower expressed, what boded in the mating weather.

"And what flower did you wear, Seyavi?"

"I, ah,—the white flower of twining (clematis), on my body and my hair, and so I sang:—

"I am the white flower of twining,
Little white flower by the river,
Oh, flower that twines close by the river;
Oh, trembling flower!
So trembles the maiden heart."

So sang Seyavi of the campoodie before she made baskets, and in her later days laid her arms upon her knees and laughed in them at the recollection. But it was not often she would say so much, never understanding the keen hunger I had for bits of lore and the "fool talk" of her people. She had fed her young son with meadowlarks' tongues, to make him quick of speech; but in late years was loath to admit it, though she had come through the period of unfaith in the lore of the clan with a fine appreciation of its beauty and significance.

"What good will your dead get, Seyavi, of the baskets you burn?" said I, coveting them for my own collection.

Thus Seyavi, "As much good as yours of the flowers you strew."

Oppapago looks on Waban, and Waban on Coso and the Bitter Lake, and the campoodie looks on these three; and more, it sees the beginning of winds along the foot of Coso, the gathering of clouds behind the high ridges, the spring flush, the soft spread of wild almond bloom on the mesa. These first, you understand, are the Paiute's walls, the other his furnishings. Not the wattled hut is his home, but the land, the winds, the hill front, the stream. These he cannot duplicate at any furbisher's shop as you who live within doors, who, if your purse allows, may have the same home at Sitka and Samarcand. So you see how it is that the homesickness of an Indian is often unto death, since he gets no relief from it; neither wind nor weed nor sky-line, nor any aspect of the hills of a strange land sufficiently like his own. So it was, when the government reached out for the Paiutes, they gathered into the Northern Reservation only such poor tribes as could devise no other end of their affairs. Here, all along the river, and south to Shoshone Land, live the clans who owned the earth, fallen into the deplorable condition of hangers-on. Yet you hear them laughing at the hour when they draw in to the campoodie after labor, when there is a smell of meat and the steam of the cooking pots goes up against the sun. Then the children lie with their toes in the ashes to hear tales; then they are merry, and have the joys of repletion and the nearness of their kind. They have their hills, and though jostled are sufficiently free to get some fortitude for what will come. For now you shall hear of the end of the basket maker.

In her best days Seyavi was most like Deborah, deep bosomed, broad in the hips, quick in counsel, slow of speech, esteemed of her people. This was that Seyavi who reared a man by her own hand, her own wit, and none other. When the townspeople began to take note of her—and it was some years after the war before there began to be any towns—she was then in the quick maturity of primitive women; but when I knew her she seemed already old. Indian women do not often live to great age, though they look incredibly steeped in years. They have the wit to win sustenance from the raw material of life without intervention, but they have not the sleek look of the women whom the social organization conspires to nourish. Seyavi had somehow squeezed out of her daily round a spiritual ichor that kept the skill in her knotted fingers long after the accustomed time, but that also failed. By all counts she would have been about sixty years old when it came her turn to sit in the dust on the sunny side of the wickiup, with little strength left for anything but looking. And in time she paid the toll of the smoky huts and became blind. This is a thing so long expected by the Paiutes that when it comes they find it neither bitter nor sweet, but tolerable because common. There were three other blind women in the campoodie, withered fruit on a bough, but they had memory and speech. By noon of the sun there were never any left in the campoodie but these or some mother of weanlings, and they sat to keep the ashes warm upon the hearth. If it were cold, they burrowed in the blankets of the hut; if it were warm, they followed the shadow of the wickiup around. Stir much out of their places they hardly dared, since one might not help another; but they called, in high, old cracked voices, gossip and reminder across the ash heaps.

Then, if they have your speech or you theirs, and have an hour to spare, there are things to be learned of life not set down in any books, folk tales, famine tales, love and long-suffering and desire, but no whimpering. Now and then one or another of the blind keepers of the camp will come across to where you sit gossiping, tapping her way among the kitchen middens, guided by your voice that carries far in the clearness and stillness of mesa afternoons. But suppose you find Seyavi retired into the privacy of her blanket, you will get nothing for that day. There is no other privacy possible in a campoodie. All the processes of life are carried on out of doors or behind the thin, twig-woven walls of the wickiup, and laughter is the only corrective for behavior. Very early the Indian learns to possess his countenance in impassivity, to cover his head with his blanket. Something to wrap around him is as necessary to the Paiute as to you your closet to pray in.

So in her blanket Seyavi, sometime basket maker, sits by the unlit hearths of her tribe and digests her life, nourishing her spirit against the time of the spirit's need, for she knows in fact quite as much of these matters as you who have a larger hope, though she has none but the certainty that having borne herself courageously to this end she will not be reborn a coyote.

The Streets of the Mountains

All streets of the mountains lead to the citadel; steep or slow they go up to the core of the hills. Any trail that goes otherwhere must dip and cross, sidle and take chances. Rifts of the hills open into each other, and the high meadows are often wide enough to be called valleys by courtesy; but one keeps this distinction in mind,—valleys are the sunken places of the earth, cañons are scored out by the glacier ploughs of God. They have a better name in the Rockies for these hill-fenced open glades of pleasantness; they call them parks. Here and there in the hill country one comes upon blind gullies fronted by high stony barriers. These head also for the heart of the mountains; their distinction is that they never get anywhere.

All mountain streets have streams to thread them, or deep grooves where a stream might run. You would do well to avoid that range uncomforted by singing floods. You will find it forsaken of most things but beauty and madness and death and God. Many such lie east and north away from the mid Sierras, and quicken the imagination with the sense of purposes not revealed, but the ordinary traveler brings nothing away from them but an intolerable thirst.

The river cañons of the Sierras of the Snows are better worth while than most Broadways, though the choice of them is like the choice of streets, not very well determined by their names. There is always an amount of local history to be read in the names of mountain highways where one touches the successive waves of occupation or discovery, as in the old villages where the neighborhoods are not built but grow. Here you have the Spanish Californian in *Cero*

Gordo and piñon; Symmes and Shepherd, pioneers both; Tunawai, probably Shoshone; Oak Creek, Kearsarge,—easy to fix the date of that christening,—Tinpah, Paiute that; Mist Cañon and Paddy Jack's. The streets of the west Sierras sloping toward the San Joaquin are long and winding, but from the east, my country, a day's ride carries one to the lake regions. The next day reaches the passes of the high divide, but whether one gets passage depends a little on how many have gone that road before, and much on one's own powers. The passes are steep and windy ridges, though not the highest. By two and three thousand feet the snow-caps overtop them. It is even possible to win through the Sierras without having passed above timber-line, but one misses a great exhilaration.

The shape of a new mountain is roughly pyramidal, running out into long shark-finned ridges that interfere and merge into other thunder-splintered sierras. You get the saw-tooth effect from a distance, but the near-by granite bulk glitters with the terrible keen polish of old glacial ages. I say terrible; so it seems. When those glossy domes swim into the alpenglow, wet after rain, you conceive how long and imperturbable are the purposes of God.

Never believe what you are told, that midsummer is the best time to go up the streets of the mountain—well—perhaps for the merely idle or sportsmanly or scientific; but for seeing and understanding, the best time is when you have the longest leave to stay. And here is a hint if you would attempt the stateliest approaches; travel light, and as much as possible live off the land. Mulligatawny soup and tinned lobster will not bring you the favor of the woodlanders.

Every cañon commends itself for some particular pleasantness; this for pines, another for trout, one for pure bleak beauty of granite buttresses, one for its far-flung irised falls; and as I say, though some are easier going, leads each to the cloud shouldering citadel. First, near the cañon mouth you get the low-heading full-branched, one-leaf pines. That is the sort of tree to know at sight, for the globose, resin-dripping cones have palatable, nourishing kernels, the main harvest of the Paiutes. That perhaps accounts for their growing accommodatingly below the limit of deep snows, grouped sombrely on the valleyward slopes. The real procession of the pines begins in the rifts with the long-leafed *Pinus Jeffreyi*, sighing its soul away upon the wind. And it ought not to sigh in such good company. Here begins the manzanita, adjusting its tortuous stiff stems to the sharp waste of boulders, its pale olive leaves twisting edgewise to the sleek, ruddy, chestnut stems; begins also the meadow-sweet, burnished laurel, and the million unregarded trumpets of the coral-red pentstemon. Wild life is likely to be busiest about the lower pine borders. One looks in hollow trees and hiving rocks for wild honey. The drone of bees, the chatter of jays, the hurry and stir of squirrels, is incessant; the air is odorous and hot. The roar of the stream fills up the morning and evening intervals, and at night the deer feed in the buckthorn thickets. It is worth watching the year round in the purlieus of the long-leafed pines. One month or another you get sight or trail of most roving mountain dwellers as they follow the limit of forbidding snows, and more bloom than you can properly appreciate.

Whatever goes up or comes down the streets of the mountains, water has the right of way; it takes the lowest ground and the shortest passage. Where the rifts are narrow, and some of the Sierra cañons are not a stone's throw from wall to wall, the best trail for foot or horse winds considerably above the watercourses; but in a country of cone-bearers there is usually a good strip of swardy sod along the cañon floor. Pine woods, the short-leafed Balfour and Murryana of the high Sierras, are sombre, rooted in the litter of a thousand years, hushed, and corrective to the spirit. The trail passes insensibly into them from the black pines and a thin belt of firs. You look back as you rise, and strain for glimpses of the tawny valley, blue glints of the Bitter Lake, and tender cloud films on the farther ranges. For such pictures the pine branches make a noble frame. Presently they close in wholly; they draw mysteriously near, covering your tracks, giving up the trail indifferently, or with a secret grudge. You get a kind of impatience with their locked ranks, until you come out lastly on some high, windy dome and see what they are about. They troop thickly up the open ways, river banks, and brook borders; up open swales of dribbling springs; swarm over old moraines; circle the peaty swamps and part and meet about clean still lakes; scale the stony gullies; tormented, bowed, persisting to the door of the storm chambers, tall priests to pray for rain. The spring winds lift clouds of pollen dust, finer than frankincense, and trail it out over high altars, staining the snow. No doubt they understand this work better than we; in fact they know no other. "Come," say the churches of the valleys, after a season of dry years, "let us pray for rain." They would do better to plant more trees.

It is a pity we have let the gift of lyric improvisation die out. Sitting islanded on some gray peak above the encompassing wood, the soul is lifted up to sing the Iliad of the pines. They have no voice but the wind, and no sound of them rises up to the high places. But the waters, the evidences of their power, that go down the steep and stony ways, the outlets of ice-bordered pools, the young rivers swaying with the force of their running, they sing and shout and trumpet at the falls, and the noise of it far outreaches the forest spires. You see from these conning towers how they call and find each other in the slender gorges; how they fumble in the meadows, needing the sheer nearing walls to give them countenance and show the way; and how the pine woods are made glad by them.

Nothing else in the streets of the mountains gives such a sense of pageantry as the conifers; other trees, if there are any, are home dwellers, like the tender fluttered, sisterhood of quaking asp. They grow in clumps by spring borders, and all their stems have a permanent curve toward the down slope, as you may also see in hillside pines, where they have borne the weight of sagging drifts.

Well up from the valley, at the confluence of cañons, are delectable summer meadows. Fireweed flames about them against the gray boulders; streams are open, go smoothly about the glacier slips and make deep bluish pools for trout. Pines raise statelier shafts and give themselves room to grow,—gentians, shinleaf, and little grass of Parnassus in their golden checkered shadows; the meadow is white with violets and all outdoors keeps the clock. For example, when the ripples at the ford of the creek raise a clear half tone,— sign that the snow water has come down from the heated high ridges,—it is time to light the evening fire. When it drops off a note—but you will not know it except the Douglas squirrel tells you with his high, fluty chirrup from the pines' aerial gloom—sign that some star watcher has caught the first far glint of the nearing sun. Whitney cries it from his vantage tower; it flashes from Oppapago to the front of Williamson; LeConte speeds it to the westering peaks. The high rills wake and run, the birds begin. But down three thousand feet in the cañon, where you stir the fire under the cooking pot, it will not be day for an hour. It goes on, the play of light across the high places, rosy, purpling, tender, glint and glow, thunder and windy flood, like the grave, exulting talk of elders above a merry game.

Who shall say what another will find most to his liking in the streets of the mountains. As for me, once set above the country of the silver firs, I must go on until I find white columbine. Around the amphitheatres of the lake regions and above them to the limit of perennial drifts they gather flock-wise in splintered rock wastes. The crowds of them, the airy spread of sepals, the pale purity of the petal spurs, the quivering swing of bloom, obsesses the sense. One must learn to spare a little of the pang of inexpressible beauty, not to spend all one's purse in one shop. There is always another year, and another.

Lingering on in the alpine regions until the first full snow, which is often before the cessation of bloom, one goes down in good company. First snows are soft and clogging and make laborious paths. Then it is the roving inhabitants range down to the edge of the wood, below the limit of early storms. Early winter and early spring one may have sight or track of deer and bear and bighorn, cougar and bobcat, about the thickets of buckthorn on open slopes between the black pines. But when the ice crust is firm above the twenty foot drifts, they range far and forage where they will. Often in midwinter will come, now and then, a long fall of soft snow piling three or four feet above the ice crust, and work a real hardship for the dwellers of these streets. When such a storm portends the weather-wise black-tail will go down across the valley and up to the pastures of Waban where no more snow falls than suffices to nourish the sparsely growing pines. But the bighorn, the wild sheep, able to bear the bitterest storms with no signs of stress, cannot cope with the loose shifty snow. Never such a storm goes over the mountains that the Indians do not catch them floundering belly deep among the lower rifts. I have a pair of horns, inconceivably heavy, that were borne as late as a year ago by a very monarch of the flock whom death overtook at the mouth of Oak Creek after a week of wet snow. He met it as a king should, with no vain effort or trembling, and it was wholly kind to take him so with four of his following rather than that the night prowlers should find him.

There is always more life abroad in the winter hills than one looks to find, and much more in evidence than in summer weather. Light feet of hare that make no print on the forest litter leave a wondrously plain track in the snow. We used to look and look at the beginning of winter for the birds to come down from the pine lands; looked in the orchard and stubble; looked north and south on the mesa for their migratory passing, and wondered that they never came. Busy little grosbeaks picked about the kitchen doors, and woodpeckers tapped the eves of the farm buildings, but we saw hardly any other of the frequenters of the summer cañons. After a while when we grew bold to tempt the snow borders we found them in the street of the mountains. In the thick pine woods where the overlapping boughs hung with snow-wreaths make wind-proof shelter tents, in a very community of dwelling, winter the bird-folk who get their living from the persisting cones and the larvae harboring bark. Ground inhabiting species seek the dim snow chambers of the chaparral. Consider how it must be in a hill-slope overgrown with stout-twigged, partly evergreen shrubs, more than man high, and as thick as a hedge. Not all the cañon's sifting of snow can fill the intricate spaces of the hill tangles. Here and there an overhanging rock, or a stiff arch of buckthorn, makes an opening to communicating rooms and runways deep under the snow.

The light filtering through the snow walls is blue and ghostly, but serves to show seeds of shrubs and grass, and berries, and the wind-built walls are warm against the wind. It seems that live plants, especially if they are evergreen and growing, give off heat; the snow wall melts earliest from within and hollows to thinness before there is a hint of spring in the air. But you think of these things afterward. Up in the street it has the effect of being done consciously; the buckthorns lean to each other and the drift to them, the little birds run in and out of their appointed ways with the greatest cheerfulness. They give almost no tokens of distress, and even if the winter tries them too much you are not to pity them. You of the house habit can hardly understand the sense of the hills. No doubt the labor of being comfortable gives you an exaggerated opinion of yourself, an exaggerated pain to be set aside. Whether the wild things understand it or not they adapt themselves to its processes with the greater ease. The business that goes on in the street of the mountain is tremendous, world-formative. Here go birds, squirrels, and red deer, children crying small wares and playing in the street, but they do not obstruct its affairs. Summer is their holiday; "Come now," says the lord of the street, "I have need of a great work and no more playing."

But they are left borders and breathing-space out of pure kindness. They are not pushed out except by the exigencies of the nobler plan which they accept with a dignity the rest of us have not yet learned.

Water Borders

I like that name the Indians give to the mountain of Lone Pine, and find it pertinent to my subject,—Oppapago, The Weeper. It sits eastward and solitary from the lordliest ranks of the Sierras, and above a range of little, old, blunt hills, and has a bowed, grave aspect as of some woman you might have known, looking out across the grassy barrows of her dead. From twin gray lakes under its noble brow stream down incessant white and tumbling waters. "Mahala all time cry," said Winnenap', drawing furrows in his rugged, wrinkled cheeks.

The origin of mountain streams is like the origin of tears, patent to the understanding but mysterious to the sense. They are always at it, but one so seldom catches them in the act. Here in the valley there is no cessation of waters even in the season when the niggard frost gives them scant leave to run. They make the most of their midday hour, and tinkle all night thinly under the ice. An ear laid to the snow catches a muffled hint of their eternal busyness fifteen or twenty feet under the cañon drifts, and long before any appreciable spring thaw, the sagging edges of the snow bridges mark out the place of their running. One who ventures to look for it finds the immediate source of the spring freshets—all the hill fronts furrowed with the reek of melting drifts, all the gravelly flats in a swirl of waters. But later, in June or July, when the camping season begins, there runs the stream away full and singing, with no visible reinforcement other than an icy trickle from some high, belated clot of snow. Oftenest the stream drops bodily from the bleak bowl of some alpine lake; sometimes breaks out of a hillside as a spring where the ear can trace it under the rubble of loose stones to the neighborhood of some blind pool. But that leaves the lakes to be accounted for.

The lake is the eye of the mountain, jade green, placid, unwinking, also unfathomable. Whatever goes on under the high and stony brows is guessed at. It is always a favorite local tradition that one or another of the blind lakes is bottomless. Often they lie in such deep cairns of broken boulders that one never gets quite to them, or gets away unhurt. One such drops below the plunging slope that the Kearsarge trail winds over, perilously, nearing the pass. It lies still and wickedly green in its sharp-lipped cup, and the guides of that region love to tell of the packs and pack animals it has swallowed up.

But the lakes of Oppapago are perhaps not so deep, less green than gray, and better befriended. The ousel haunts them, while still hang about their coasts the thin undercut drifts that never quite leave the high altitudes. In and out of the bluish ice caves he flits and sings, and his singing heard from above is sweet and uncanny like the Nixie's chord. One finds butterflies, too, about these high, sharp regions which might be called desolate, but will not by me who love them. This is above timber-line but not too high for comforting by succulent small herbs and golden tufted grass. A granite mountain does not crumble with alacrity, but once resolved to soil makes the best of it. Every handful of loose gravel not wholly water leached affords a plant footing, and even in such unpromising surroundings there is a choice of locations. There is never going to be any communism of mountain herbage, their affinities are too sure. Full in the runnels of snow water on gravelly, open spaces in the shadow of a drift, one looks to find buttercups, frozen knee-deep by night, and owning no desire but to ripen their fruit above the icy bath. Soppy little plants of the portulaca and small, fine ferns shiver under the drip of falls and in dribbling crevices. The bleaker the situation, so it is near a stream border, the better the cassiope loves it. Yet I have not found it on the polished glacier slips, but where the country rock cleaves and splinters in the high windy headlands that the wild sheep frequents, hordes and hordes of the white bells swing over matted, mossy foliage. On Oppapago, which is also called Sheep Mountain, one finds not far from the beds of cassiope the ice-worn, stony hollows where the bighorns cradle their young. These are above the wolf's quest and the eagle's wont, and though the heather beds are softer, they are neither so dry nor so warm, and here only the stars go by. No other animal of any pretensions makes a habitat of the alpine regions. Now and then one gets a hint of some small, brown creature, rat or mouse kind, that slips secretly among the rocks; no others adapt themselves to desertness of aridity or altitude so readily as these ground inhabiting, graminivorous species. If there is an open stream the trout go up the lake as far as the water breeds food for them, but the ousel goes farthest, for pure love of it.

Since no lake can be at the highest point, it is possible to find plant life higher than the water borders; grasses perhaps the highest, gilias, royal blue trusses of polymonium, rosy plats of Sierra primroses. What one has to get used to in flowers at high altitudes is the bleaching of the sun. Hardly do they hold their virgin color for a day, and this early fading before their function is performed gives them a pitiful appearance not according with their hardihood. The color scheme runs along the high ridges from blue to rosy purple, carmine and coral red; along the water borders it is chiefly white and yellow where the mimulus makes a vivid note, running into red when the two schemes meet and mix about the borders of the meadows, at the upper limit of the columbine.

Here is the fashion in which a mountain stream gets down from the perennial pastures of the snow to its proper level and identity as an irrigating ditch. It slips stilly by the glacier scoured rim of an ice bordered pool, drops over sheer, broken ledges to another pool, gathers itself, plunges headlong on a rocky ripple slope, finds a lake again, reinforced, roars downward to a pot-hole, foams and bridles, glides a tranquil reach in some still meadow, tumbles into a sharp groove between hill flanks, curdles under the stream tangles, and so arrives at the open country and steadier going. Meadows, little strips of alpine freshness, begin before the timber-line is reached. Here one treads on a carpet of dwarf willows, downy catkins of creditable size and the greatest economy of foliage and stems. No other plant of high altitudes knows its business so well.

It hugs the ground, grows roots from stem joints where no roots should be, grows a slender leaf or two and twice as many erect full catkins that rarely, even in that short growing season, fail of fruit. Dipping over banks in the inlets of the creeks, the fortunate find the rosy apples of the miniature manzanita, barely, but always quite sufficiently, borne above the spongy sod. It does not do to be anything but humble in the alpine regions, but not fearful. I have pawed about for hours in the chill sward of meadows where one might properly expect to get one's death, and got no harm from it, except it might be Oliver Twist's complaint. One comes soon after this to shrubby willows, and where willows are trout may be confidently looked for in most Sierra streams. There is no accounting for their distribution; though provident anglers have assisted nature of late, one still comes upon roaring brown waters where trout might very well be, but are not.

The highest limit of conifers—in the middle Sierras, the white bark pine—is not along the water border. They come to it about the level of the heather, but they have no such affinity for dampness as the tamarack pines. Scarcely any birdnote breaks the stillness of the timber-line, but chipmunks inhabit here, as may be guessed by the gnawed ruddy cones of the pines, and lowering hours the woodchucks come down to the water. On a little spit of land running into Windy Lake we found one summer the evidence of a tragedy; a pair of sheep's horns not fully grown caught in the crotch of a pine where the living sheep must have lodged them. The trunk of the tree had quite closed over them, and the skull bones crumbled away from the weathered horn cases. We hoped it was not too far out of the running of night prowlers to have put a speedy end to the long agony, but we could not be sure. I never liked the spit of Windy Lake again.

It seems that all snow nourished plants count nothing so excellent in their kind as to be forehanded with their bloom, working secretly to that end under the high piled winters. The heathers begin by the lake borders, while little sodden drifts still shelter under their branches. I have seen the tiniest of them (*Kalmia glauca*) blooming, and with well-formed fruit, a foot away from a snowbank from which it could hardly have emerged within a week. Somehow the soul of the heather has entered into the blood of the English-speaking. "And oh! is that heather?" they say; and the

most indifferent ends by picking a sprig of it in a hushed, wonder-
ing way. One must suppose that the root of their respective races
issued from the glacial borders at about the same epoch, and
remember their origin.

Among the pines where the slope of the land allows it, the
streams run into smooth, brown, trout-abounding rills across open
flats that are in reality filled lake basins. These are the displaying
grounds of the gentians—blue—blue—eye-blue, perhaps, virtuous
and likable flowers. One is not surprised to learn that they have
tonic properties. But if your meadow should be outside the forest
reserve, and the sheep have been there, you will find little but the
shorter, paler G. Newberryii, and in the matted sods of the little
tongues of greenness that lick up among the pines along the watercourses, white, scentless, nearly stemless, alpine violets.

At about the nine thousand foot level and in the summer there
will be hosts of rosy-winged dodecatheon, called shooting-stars,
outlining the crystal runnels in the sod. Single flowers have often a
two-inch spread of petal, and the full, twelve blossomed heads
above the slender pedicels have the airy effect of wings.

It is about this level one looks to find the largest lakes with thick
ranks of pines bearing down on them, often swamped in the summer floods and paying the inevitable penalty for such encroach-
ment. Here in wet coves of the hills harbors that crowd of bloom
that makes the wonder of the Sierra cañons.

They drift under the alternate flicker and gloom of the windy
rooms of pines, in gray rock shelters, and by the ooze of blind
springs, and their juxtapositions are the best imaginable. Lilies
come up out of fern beds, columbine swings over meadow-sweet,
white rein-orchids quake in the leaning grass. Open swales, where
in wet years may be running water, are plantations of false hellebore (Veratrum Californicum), tall, branched candelabra of greenish
bloom above the sessile, sheathing, boat-shaped leaves, semi-
translucent in the sun. A stately plant of the lily family, but why
"false?" It is frankly offensive in its character, and its young juices
deadly as any hellebore that ever grew.

Like most mountain herbs it has an uncanny haste to bloom.
One hears by night, when all the wood is still, the crepitatious

rustle of the unfolding leaves and the pushing flower-stalk within, that has open blossoms before it has fairly uncramped from the sheath. It commends itself by a certain exclusiveness of growth, taking enough room and never elbowing; for if the flora of the lake region has a fault it is that there is too much of it. We have more than three hundred species from Kearsarge Cañon alone, and if that does not include them all it is because they were already collected otherwhere.

One expects to find lakes down to about nine thousand feet, leading into each other by comparatively open ripple slopes and white cascades. Below the lakes are filled basins that are still spongy swamps, or substantial meadows, as they get down and down.

Here begin the stream tangles. On the east slopes of the middle Sierras the pines, all but an occasional yellow variety, desert the stream borders about the level of the lowest lakes, and the birches and tree-willows begin. The firs hold on almost to the mesa levels,—there are no foothills on this eastern slope,—and whoever has firs misses nothing else. It goes without saying that a tree that can afford to take fifty years to its first fruiting will repay acquaintance. It keeps, too, all that half century, a virginal grace of outline, but having once flowered, begins quietly to put away the things of its youth. Year by year the lower rounds of boughs are shed, leaving no scar; year by year the star-branched minarets approach the sky. A fir-tree loves a water border, loves a long wind in a draughty cañon, loves to spend itself secretly on the inner finishings of its burnished, shapely cones. Broken open in mid-season the petal-shaped scales show a crimson satin surface, perfect as a rose.

The birch—the brown-bark western birch characteristic of lower stream tangles—is a spoil sport. It grows thickly to choke the stream that feeds it; grudges it the sky and space for angler's rod and fly. The willows do better; painted-cup, cypripedium, and the hollow stalks of span-broad white umbels, find a footing among their stems. But in general the steep plunges, the white swirls, green and tawny pools, the gliding hush of waters between the meadows and the mesas afford little fishing and few flowers.

One looks for these to begin again when once free of the rifted cañon walls; the high note of babble and laughter falls off to the steadier mellow tone of a stream that knows its purpose and reflects the sky.

Other Water Borders

It is the proper destiny of every considerable stream in the west to become an irrigating ditch. It would seem the streams are willing. They go as far as they can, or dare, toward the tillable lands in their own boulder fenced gullies—but how much farther in the man-made waterways. It is difficult to come into intimate relations with appropriated waters; like very busy people they have no time to reveal themselves. One needs to have known an irrigating ditch when it was a brook, and to have lived by it, to mark the morning and evening tone of its crooning, rising and falling to the excess of snow water; to have watched far across the valley, south to the Eclipse and north to the Twisted Dyke, the shining wall of the village water gate; to see still blue herons stalking the little glinting weirs across the field.

Perhaps to get into the mood of the waterways one needs to have seen old Amos Judson asquat on the headgate with his gun, guarding his water-right toward the end of a dry summer. Amos owned the half of Tule Creek and the other half pertained to the neighboring Greenfields ranch. Years of a "short water crop," that is, when too little snow fell on the high pine ridges, or, falling, melted too early, Amos held that it took all the water that came down to make his half, and maintained it with a Winchester and a deadly aim. Jesus Montaña, first proprietor of Greenfields,—you can see at once that Judson had the racial advantage,—contesting the right with him, walked into five of Judson's bullets and his eternal possessions on the same occasion. That was the Homeric age of settlement and passed into tradition. Twelve years later one of the Clarks, holding Greenfields, not so very green by now, shot one of the

Judsons. Perhaps he hoped that also might become classic, but the
jury found for manslaughter. It had the effect of discouraging the
Greenfields claim, but Amos used to sit on the headgate just the
same, as quaint and lone a figure as the sandhill crane watching for
water toads below the Tule drop. Every subsequent owner of
Greenfields bought it with Amos in full view. The last of these was
Diedrick. Along in August of that year came a week of low water.
Judson's ditch failed and he went out with his rifle to learn why.
There on the headgate sat Diedrick's frau with a long-handled
shovel across her lap and all the water turned into Diedrick's ditch;
there she sat knitting through the long sun, and the children
brought out her dinner. It was all up with Amos; he was too much
of a gentleman to fight a lady—that was the way he expressed it.
She was a very large lady, and a long-handled shovel is no mean
weapon. The next year Judson and Diedrick put in a modern water
gauge and took the summer ebb in equal inches. Some of the water-
right difficulties are more squalid than this, some more tragic; but
unless you have known them you cannot very well know what the
water thinks as it slips past the gardens and in the long slow sweeps
of the canal. You get that sense of brooding from the confined and
sober floods, not all at once but by degrees, as one might become
aware of a middle-aged and serious neighbor who has had that in
his life to make him so. It is the repose of the completely accepted
instinct.

With the water runs a certain following of thirsty herbs and
shrubs. The willows go as far as the stream goes, and a bit farther on
the slightest provocation. They will strike root in the leak of a
flume, or the dribble of an overfull bank, coaxing the water beyond
its appointed bounds. Given a new waterway in a barren land, and
in three years the willows have fringed all its miles of banks;
three years more and they will touch tops across it. It is perhaps
due to the early usurpation of the willows that so little else finds
growing-room along the large canals. The birch beginning far
back in the cañon tangles is more conservative; it is shy of man
haunts and needs to have the permanence of its drink assured. It
stops far short of the summer limit of waters, and I have never
known it to take up a position on the banks beyond the ploughed

lands. There is something almost like premeditation in the avoidance of cultivated tracts by certain plants of water borders. The clematis, mingling its foliage secretly with its host, comes down with the stream tangles to the village fences, skips over to corners of little used pasture lands and the plantations that spring up about waste water pools; but never ventures a footing in the trail of spade or plough; will not be persuaded to grow in any garden plot. On the other hand, the horehound, the common European species imported with the colonies, hankers after hedgerows and snug little borders. It is more widely distributed than many native species, and may be always found along the ditches in the village corners, where it is not appreciated. The irrigating ditch is an impartial distributer. It gathers all the alien weeds that come west in garden and grass seeds and affords them harbor in its banks. There one finds the European mallow (*Malva rotundifolia*) spreading out to the streets with the summer overflow, and every spring a dandelion or two, brought in with the blue grass seed, uncurls in the swardy soil. Farther than either of these have come the lilies that the Chinese coolies cultivate in adjacent mud holes for their foodful bulbs. The *seegoo* establishes itself very readily in swampy borders, and the white blossom spikes among the arrow-pointed leaves are quite as acceptable to the eye as any native species.

In the neighborhood of towns founded by the Spanish Californians, whether this plant is native to the locality or not, one can always find aromatic clumps of *yerba buena*, the "good herb" (*Micromeria Douglassii*). The virtue of it as a febrifuge was taught to the mission fathers by the neophytes, and wise old dames of my acquaintance have worked astonishing cures with it and the succulent *yerba mansa*. This last is native to wet meadows and distinguished enough to have a family all to itself.

Where the irrigating ditches are shallow and a little neglected, they choke quickly with watercress that multiplies about the lowest Sierra springs. It is characteristic of the frequenters of water borders near man haunts, that they are chiefly of the sorts that are useful to man, as if they made their services an excuse for the intrusion. The joint-grass of soggy pastures produces edible, nut-flavored tubers, called by the Indians *taboose*. The common reed of the ultramontane marshes (here *Phragmites vulgaris*), a very stately, whispering reed, light and strong for shafts or arrows, affords sweet sap and pith which makes a passable sugar.

It seems the secrets of plant powers and influences yield themselves most readily to primitive peoples, at least one never hears of the knowledge coming from any other source. The Indian never concerns himself, as the botanist and the poet, with the plant's appearances and relations, but with what it can do for him. It can do much, but how do you suppose he finds it out; what instincts or accidents guide him? How does a cat know when to eat catnip? Why do western bred cattle avoid loco weed, and strangers eat it and go mad? One might suppose that in a time of famine the Paiutes digged wild parsnip in meadow corners and died from eating it, and so learned to produce death swiftly and at will. But how did they learn, repenting in the last agony, that animal fat is the best antidote for its virulence; and who taught them that the essence of joint pine (*Ephedra nevadensis*), which looks to have no juice in it of any sort, is efficacious in stomachic disorders. But they so understand and so use. One believes it to be a sort of instinct atrophied by disuse in a complexer civilization. I remember very well when I came first upon a wet meadow of *yerba mansa*, not knowing its name or use. It *looked* potent; the cool, shiny leaves, the succulent, pink stems and fruity bloom. A little touch, a hint, a word, and I should have known what use to put them to. So I felt, unwilling to leave it until we had come to an understanding. So a musician might have felt in the presence of an instrument known to be within his province, but beyond his power. It was with the relieved sense of having shaped a long surmise that I watched the Señora Romero make a poultice of it for my burned hand.

On, down from the lower lakes to the village weirs, the brown and golden disks of *helenum* have beauty as a sufficient excuse for being. The plants anchor out on tiny capes, or mid-stream islets, with the nearly sessile radicle leaves submerged. The flowers keep up a constant trepidation in time with the hasty water beating at their stems, a quivering, instinct with life, that seems always at the point of breaking into flight; just as the babble of the watercourses always approaches articulation but never quite achieves it.

Although of wide range the *helenum* never makes itself common through profusion, and may be looked for in the same places from year to year. Another lake dweller that comes down to the ploughed lands is the red columbine (*C. truncata*). It requires no encouragement other than shade, but grows too rank in the summer heats and loses its wildwood grace. A common enough orchid in these parts is the false lady's slipper (*Epipactis gigantea*), one that springs up by any water where there is sufficient growth of other sorts to give it countenance. It seems to thrive best in an atmosphere of suffocation.

The middle Sierras fall off abruptly eastward toward the high valleys. Peaks of the fourteen thousand class, belted with sombre swathes of pine, rise almost directly from the bench lands with no foothill approaches. At the lower edge of the bench or mesa the land falls away, often by a fault, to the river hollows, and along the drop one looks for springs or intermittent swampy swales. Here the plant world resembles a little the lake gardens, modified by altitude and the use the town folk put it to for pasture. Here are cress, blue violets, potentilla, and, in the damp of the willow fence-rows, white false asphodels. I am sure we make too free use of this word *false* in naming plants—false mallow, false lupine, and the like. The asphodel is at least no falsifier, but a true lily by all the heaven-set marks, though small of flower and run mostly to leaves, and should have a name that gives it credit for growing up in such celestial semblance. Native to the mesa meadows is a pale iris, gardens of it acres wide, that in the spring season of full bloom make an airy fluttering as of azure wings. Single flowers are too thin and sketchy of outline to affect the imagination, but the full fields have the misty blue of mirage waters rolled across desert sand, and quicken the senses to the anticipation of things ethereal. A very poet's flower, I thought; not fit for gathering up, and proving a nuisance in the pastures, therefore needing to be the more loved. And one day I caught Winnenap' drawing out from mid leaf a fine strong fibre for making snares. The borders of the iris fields are pure gold, nearly sessile buttercups and a creeping-stemmed composite of a redder hue. I am convinced that English-speaking children will always have buttercups. If they do not light upon the original companion of little frogs they will take the next best and cherish it accordingly. I find five unrelated species loved by that name, and as many more and as inappropriately called cowslips.

By every mesa spring one may expect to find a single shrub of the buckthorn, called of old time *Cascara sagrada*—the sacred bark. Up in the cañons, within the limit of the rains, it seeks rather a stony slope, but in the dry valleys is not found away from water borders.

In all the valleys and along the desert edges of the west are considerable areas of soil sickly with alkali-collecting pools, black and evil-smelling like old blood. Very little grows hereabout but thick-leaved pickle weed. Curiously enough, in this stiff mud, along roadways where there is frequently a little leakage from canals, grows the only western representative of the true heliotropes (*Heliotropium curassavicum*). It has flowers of faded white, foliage of faded green, resembling the "live-for-ever" of old gardens and graveyards, but even less attractive. After so much schooling in the virtues of water-seeking plants, one is not surprised to learn that its mucilaginous sap has healing powers.

Last and inevitable resort of overflow waters is the tulares, great wastes of reeds (*Juncus*) in sickly, slow streams. The reeds, called tules, are ghostly pale in winter, in summer deep poisonous-looking green, the waters thick and brown; the reed beds breaking into dingy pools, clumps of rotting willows, narrow winding water lanes and sinking paths. The tules grow inconceivably thick in places, standing man-high above the water; cattle, no, not any fish nor fowl can penetrate them. Old stalks succumb slowly; the bed soil is quagmire, settling with the weight as it fills and fills. Too slowly for counting they raise little islands from the bog and reclaim the land. The waters pushed out cut deeper channels, gnaw off the edges of the solid earth.

The tulares are full of mystery and malaria. That is why we have meant to explore them and have never done so. It must be a happy mystery. So you would think to hear the redwinged blackbirds proclaim it clear March mornings. Flocks of them, and every flock a myriad, shelter in the dry, whispering stems. They make little arched runways deep into the heart of the tule beds. Miles across the valley one hears the clamor of their high, keen flutings in the mating weather.

Wild fowl, quacking hordes of them, nest in the tulares. Any day's venture will raise from open shallows the great blue heron on his hollow wings. Chill evenings the mallard drakes cry continually from the glassy pools, the bittern's hollow boom rolls along the water paths. Strange and far-flown fowl drop down against the saffron, autumn sky. All day wings beat above it hazy with speed; long flights of cranes glimmer in the twilight. By night one wakes to hear the clanging geese go over. One wishes for, but gets no nearer speech from those the reedy fens have swallowed up. What they do there, how fare, what find, is the secret of the tulares.

Nurslings of the Sky

Choose a hill country for storms. There all the business of the weather is carried on above your horizon and loses its terror in familiarity. When you come to think about it, the disastrous storms are on the levels, sea or sand or plains. There you get only a hint of what is about to happen, the fume of the gods rising from their meeting place under the rim of the world; and when it breaks upon you there is no stay nor shelter. The terrible mewings and mouthings of a Kansas wind have the added terror of viewlessness. You are lapped in them like uprooted grass; suspect them of a personal grudge. But the storms of hill countries have other business. They scoop watercourses, manure the pines, twist them to a finer fibre, fit the firs to be masts and spars, and, if you keep reasonably out of the track of their affairs, do you no harm.

They have habits to be learned, appointed paths, seasons, and warnings, and they leave you in no doubt about their performances. One who builds his house on a water scar or the rubble of a steep slope must take chances. So they did in Overtown who built in the wash of Argus water, and at Kearsarge at the foot of a steep, treeless swale. After twenty years Argus water rose in the wash against the frail houses, and the piled snows of Kearsarge slid down at a thunder peal over the cabins and the camp, but you could conceive that it was the fault of neither the water nor the snow.

The first effect of cloud study is a sense of presence and intention in storm processes. Weather does not happen. It is the visible manifestation of the Spirit moving itself in the void. It gathers itself together under the heavens; rains, snows, yearns mightily in wind, smiles; and the Weather Bureau, situated advantageously for that very business, taps the record on his instruments and going out on the streets denies his God, not having gathered the sense of what he has seen. Hardly anybody takes account of the fact that John Muir, who knows more of mountain storms than any other, is a devout man.

Of the high Sierras choose the neighborhood of the splintered peaks about the Kern and King's river divide for storm study, or the short, wide-mouthed cañons opening eastward on high valleys. Days when the hollows are steeped in a warm, winey flood the clouds come walking on the floor of heaven, flat and pearly gray beneath, rounded and pearly white above. They gather flock-wise, moving on the level currents that roll about the peaks, lock hands and settle with the cooler air, drawing a veil about those places where they do their work. If their meeting or parting takes place at sunrise or sunset, as it often does, one gets the splendor of the apocalypse. There will be cloud pillars miles high, snow-capped, glorified, and preserving an orderly perspective before the unbarred door of the sun, or perhaps mere ghosts of clouds that dance to some pied piper of an unfelt wind. But be it day or night, once they have settled to their work, one sees from the valley only the blank wall of their tents stretched along the ranges. To get the real effect of a mountain storm you must be inside.

One who goes often into a hill country learns not to say: What if it should rain? It always does rain somewhere among the peaks: the unusual thing is that one should escape it. You might suppose that if you took any account of plant contrivances to save their pollen powder against showers. Note how many there are deep-throated and bell-flowered like the pentstemons, how many have nodding pedicels as the columbine, how many grow in copse shelters and grow there only. There is keen delight in the quick showers of summer cañons, with the added comfort, born of experience, of knowing that no harm comes of a wetting at high altitudes. The day is warm; a white cloud spies over the cañon wall, slips up behind the ridge to cross it by some windy pass, obscures your sun. Next you hear the rain drum on the broad-leaved hellebore, and beat down the mimulus beside the brook. You shelter on the lee of some strong pine with shut-winged butterflies and merry, fiddling creatures of the wood. Runnels of rain water from the glacier-slips swirl through the pine needles into rivulets; the streams froth and rise in their banks. The sky is white with cloud; the sky is gray with rain; the sky is clear. The summer showers leave no wake.

Such as these follow each other day by day for weeks in August weather. Sometimes they chill suddenly into wet snow that packs about the lake gardens clear to the blossom frills, and melts away harmlessly. Sometimes one has the good fortune from a heather-grown headland to watch a rain-cloud forming in mid-air. Out over meadow or lake region begins a little darkling of the sky,—no cloud, no wind, just a smokiness such as spirits materialize from in witch stories.

It rays out and draws to it some floating films from secret cañons. Rain begins, "slow dropping veil of thinnest lawn;" a wind comes up and drives the formless thing across a meadow, or a dull lake pitted by the glancing drops, dissolving as it drives. Such rains relieve like tears.

The same season brings the rains that have work to do, ploughing storms that alter the face of things. These come with thunder and the play of live fire along the rocks. They come with great winds that try the pines for their work upon the seas and strike out the unfit. They shake down avalanches of splinters from sky-line pinnacles and raise up sudden floods like battle fronts in the cañons against towns, trees, and boulders. They would be kind if they could, but have more important matters. Such storms, called cloud-bursts by the country folk, are not rain, rather the spillings of Thor's cup, jarred by the Thunderer. After such a one the water that comes up in the village hydrants miles away is white with forced bubbles from the wind-tormented streams.

All that storms do to the face of the earth you may read in the geographies, but not what they do to our contemporaries. I remember one night of thunderous rain made unendurably mournful by the houseless cry of a cougar whose lair, and perhaps his family, had been buried under a slide of broken boulders on the slope of Kearsarge. We had heard the heavy denotation of the slide about the hour of the alpenglow, a pale rosy interval in a darkling air, and judged he must have come from hunting to the ruined cliff and paced the night out before it, crying a very human woe. I remember, too, in that same season of storms, a lake made milky white for days, and crowded out of its bed by clay washed into it by a fury of rain, with the trout floating in it belly up, stunned by the shock of the sudden flood. But there were trout enough for what was left of the lake next year and the beginning of a meadow about its upper rim. What taxed me most in the wreck of one of my favorite cañons by cloud-burst was to see a bobcat mother mouthing her drowned kittens in the ruined lair built in the wash, far above the limit of accustomed waters, but not far enough for the unexpected. After a time you get the point of view of gods about these things to save you from being too pitiful.

The great snows that come at the beginning of winter, before there is yet any snow except the perpetual high banks, are best worth while to watch. These come often before the late bloomers are gone and while the migratory birds are still in the piney woods. Down in the valley you see little but the flocking of blackbirds in the streets, or the low flight of mallards over the tulares, and the gathering of clouds behind Williamson. First there is a waiting stillness in the wood; the pine-trees creak although there is no wind, the sky glowers, the firs rock by the water borders. The noise of the creek rises insistently and falls off a full note like a child abashed by sudden silence in the room. This changing of the stream-tone following tardily the changes of the sun on melting snows is most meaningful of wood notes. After it runs a little trumpeter wind to cry the wild creatures to their holes. Sometimes the warning hangs in the air for days with increasing stillness. Only Clark's crow and the strident jays make light of it; only they can afford to. The cattle get down to the foothills and ground inhabiting creatures make fast their doors. It grows chill, blind clouds fumble in the cañons; there will be a roll of thunder, perhaps, or a flurry of rain, but mostly the snow is born in the air with quietness and the sense of strong white pinions softly stirred. It increases, is wet and clogging, and makes a white night of midday.

There is seldom any wind with first snows, more often rain, but later, when there is already a smooth foot or two over all the slopes, the drifts begin. The late snows are fine and dry, mere ice granules

at the wind's will. Keen mornings after a storm they are blown out
in wreaths and banners from the high ridges sifting into the
cañons.

Once in a year or so we have a "big snow." The cloud tents are
widened out to shut in the valley and an outlying range or two and
are drawn tight against the sun. Such a storm begins warm, with a
dry white mist that fills and fills between the ridges, and the air is
thick with formless groaning. Now for days you get no hint of the
neighboring ranges until the snows begin to lighten and some
shouldering peak lifts through a rent. Mornings after the heavy
snows are steely blue, two-edged with cold, divinely fresh and still,
and these are times to go up to the pine borders. There you may find
floundering in the unstable drifts "tainted wethers" of the wild
sheep, faint from age and hunger; easy prey. Even the deer make
slow going in the thick fresh snow, and once we found a wolverine
going blind and feebly in the white glare.

No tree takes the snow stress with such ease as the silver fir. The
star-whorled, fan-spread branches droop under the soft wreaths—
droop and press flatly to the trunk; presently the point of overload-
ing is reached, there is a soft sough and muffled dropping, the boughs
recover, and the weighting goes on until the drifts have reached the
midmost whorls and covered up the branches. When the snows are
particularly wet and heavy they spread over the young firs in green-
ribbed tents wherein harbor winter loving birds.

All storms of desert hills, except wind storms, are impotent. East
and east of the Sierras they rise in nearly parallel ranges, desertward, and no rain breaks over them, except from some far-strayed
cloud or roving wind from the California Gulf, and these only in
winter. In summer the sky travails with thunderings and the flare
of sheet lightnings to win a few blistering big drops, and once in a
lifetime the chance of a torrent. But you have not known what force
resides in the mindless things until you have known a desert wind.
One expects it at the turn of the two seasons, wet and dry, with elec-
trified tense nerves. Along the edge of the mesa where it drops off to
the valley, dust devils begin to rise white and steady, fanning out at
the top like the genii out of the Fisherman's bottle. One supposes the
Indians might have learned the use of smoke signals from these

dust pillars as they learn most things direct from the tutelage of the earth. The air begins to move fluently, blowing hot and cold between the ranges. Far south rises a murk of sand against the sky; it grows, the wind shakes itself, and has a smell of earth. The cloud of small dust takes on the color of gold and shuts out the neighborhood, the push of the wind is unsparing. Only man of all folk is foolish enough to stir abroad in it. But being in a house is really much worse; no relief from the dust, and a great fear of the creaking timbers. There is no looking ahead in such a wind, and the bite of the small sharp sand on exposed skin is keener than any insect sting. One might sleep, for the lapping of the wind wears one to the point of exhaustion very soon, but there is dread, in open sand stretches sometimes justified, of being over blown by the drift. It is hot, dry, fretful work, but by going along the ground with the wind behind, one may come upon strange things in its tumultuous privacy. I like these truces of wind and heat that the desert makes, otherwise I do not know how I should come by so many acquaintances with furtive folk. I like to see hawks sitting daunted in shallow holes, not daring to spread a feather, and doves in a row by the prickle bushes, and shut-eyed cattle, turned tail to the wind in a patient doze. I like the smother of sand among the dunes, and finding small coiled snakes in open places, but I never like to come in a wind upon the silly sheep. The wind robs them of what wit they had, and they seem never to have learned the self-induced hypnotic stupor with which most wild things endure weather stress. I have never heard that the desert winds brought harm to any other than the wandering shepherds and their flocks. Once below Pastaria Little Pete showed me bones sticking out of the sand where a flock of two hundred had been smothered in a bygone wind. In many places the four-foot posts of a cattle fence had been buried by the wind-blown dunes.

It is enough occupation, when no storm is brewing, to watch the cloud currents and the chambers of the sky. From Kearsarge, say, you look over Inyo and find pink soft cloud masses asleep on the level desert air; south of you hurries a white troop late to some gathering of their kind at the back of Oppapago; nosing the foot of Waban, a woolly mist creeps south. In the clean, smooth paths of the middle sky and highest up in air, drift, unshepherded, small flocks ranging contrarily. You will find the proper names of these things in the reports of the Weather Bureau—cirrus, cumulus, and the like—and charts that will teach by study when to sow and take up crops. It is astonishing the trouble men will be at to find out when to plant potatoes, and gloze over the eternal meaning of the skies. You have to beat out for yourself many mornings on the windly headlands the sense of the fact that you get the same rainbow in the cloud drift over Waban and the spray of your garden hose. And not necessarily then do you live up to it.

The Little Town of the Grape Vines

There are still some places in the west where the quails cry *"cuidado"*; where all the speech is soft, all the manners gentle; where all the dishes have *chile* in them, and they make more of the Sixteenth of September than they do of the Fourth of July. I mean in particular El Pueblo de Las Uvas. Where it lies, how to come at it, you will not get from me; rather would I show you the heron's nest in the tulares. It has a peak behind it, glinting above the tamarack pines, above a breaker of ruddy hills that have a long slope valley-wards and the shoreward steep of waves toward the Sierras.

Below the Town of the Grape Vines, which shortens to Las Uvas for common use, the land dips away to the river pastures and the tulares. It shrouds under a twilight thicket of vines, under a dome of cottonwood-trees, drowsy and murmurous as a hive. Hereabouts are some strips of tillage and the headgates that dam up the creek for the village weirs; upstream you catch the growl of the arrastra. Wild vines that begin among the willows lap over to the orchard rows, take the trellis and rooftree.

There is another town above Las Uvas that merits some attention, a town of arches and airy crofts, full of linnets, blackbirds, fruit birds, small sharp hawks, and mockingbirds that sing by night. They pour out piercing, unendurably sweet cavatinas above the fragrance of bloom and musky smell of fruit. Singing is in fact the business of the night at Las Uvas as sleeping is for midday. When the moon comes over the mountain wall new-washed from the sea, and the shadows lie like lace on the stamped floors of the patios, from recess to recess of the vine tangle runs the thrum of guitars and the voice of singing.

At Las Uvas they keep up all the good customs brought out of Old Mexico or bred in a lotus-eating land; drink, and are merry and look out for something to eat afterward; have children, nine or ten to a family, have cock-fights, keep the siesta, smoke cigarettes and wait for the sun to go down. And always they dance; at dusk on the smooth adobe floors, afternoons under the trellises where the earth is damp and has a fruity smell. A betrothal, a wedding, or a christening, or the mere proximity of a guitar is sufficient occasion; and if the occasion lacks, send for the guitar and dance anyway.

All this requires explanation. Antonio Sevadra, drifting this way from Old Mexico with the flood that poured into the Tappan district after the first notable strike, discovered La Golondrina. It was a generous lode and Tony a good fellow; to work it he brought in all the Sevadras, even to the twice-removed; all the Castros who were his wife's family, all the Saises, Romeros, and Eschobars,—the relations of his relations-in-law. There you have the beginning of a pretty considerable town. To these accrued much of the Spanish California float swept out of the southwest by eastern enterprise. They slacked away again when the price of silver went down, and the ore dwindled in La Golondrina. All the hot eddy of mining life swept away from that corner of the hills, but there were always those too idle, too poor to move, or too easily content with El Pueblo de Las Uvas.

Nobody comes nowadays to the town of the grape vines except, as we say, "with the breath of crying," but of these enough. All the low sills run over with small heads. Ah, ah! There is a kind of pride in that if you did but know it, to have your baby every year or so as the time sets, and keep a full breast. So great a blessing as marriage is easily come by. It is told of Ruy Garcia that when he went for his marriage license he lacked a dollar of the clerk's fee, but borrowed it of the sheriff, who expected reëlection and exhibited thereby a commendable thrift.

Of what account is it to lack meal or meat when you may have it of any neighbor? Besides, there is sometimes a point of honor in these things. Jesus Romero, father of ten, had a job sacking ore in the Marionette which he gave up of his own accord. "Eh, why?" said Jesus, "for my fam'ly."

"It is so, señora," he said solemnly, "I go to the Marionette, I work, I eat meat—pie—frijoles—good, ver' good. I come home sad'day nigh' I see my fam'ly. I play lil' game poker with the boys, have lil' drink wine, my money all gone. My family have no money, nothing eat. All time I work at mine I eat, good, ver' good grub. I think sorry for my fam'ly. No, no, señora, I no work no more that Marionette, I stay with my fam'ly." The wonder of it is, I think, that the family had the same point of view.

Every house in the town of the vines has its garden plot, corn and brown beans and a row of peppers reddening in the sun; and in damp borders of the irrigating ditches clumps of *yerba santa*, horehound, catnip, and spikenard, wholesome herbs and curative, but if no peppers then nothing at all. You will have for a holiday dinner, in Las Uvas, soup with meat balls and chile in it, chicken with chile, rice with chile, fried beans with more chile, enchilada, which is corn cake with a sauce of chile and tomatoes, onion, grated cheese, and olives, and for a relish chile *tepines* passed about in a dish, all of which is comfortable and corrective to the stomach. You will have wine which every man makes for himself, of good body and inimitable bouquet, and sweets that are not nearly so nice as they look.

There are two occasions when you may count on that kind of a meal; always on the Sixteenth of September, and on the two-yearly visits of Father Shannon. It is absurd, of course, that El Pueblo de Las Uvas should have an Irish priest, but Black Rock, Minton, Jimville, and all that country round do not find it so. Father Shannon visits them all, waits by the Red Butte to confess the shepherds who go through with their flocks, carries blessing to small and isolated mines, and so in the course of a year or so works around to Las Uvas to bury and marry and christen. Then all the little graves in the *Campo Santo* are brave with tapers, the brown pine headboards blossom like Aaron's rod with paper roses and bright cheap prints of Our Lady of Sorrows. Then the Señora Sevadra, who thinks herself elect of heaven for that office, gathers up the original sinners, the little Elijias, Lolas, Manuelitas, Josés, and Felipés, by dint of adjurations and sweets smuggled into small perspiring palms, to fit them for the Sacrament.

I used to peek in at them, never so softly, in Doña Ina's living-room; Raphael-eyed little imps, going sidewise on their knees to rest them from the bare floor, candles lit on the mantel to give a religious air, and a great sheaf of wild bloom before the Holy Family. Come Sunday they set out the altar in the schoolhouse, with the fine-drawn altar cloths, the beaten silver candlesticks, and the wax images, chief glory of Las Uvas, brought up mule-back from Old Mexico forty years ago. All in white the communicants go up two and two in a hushed, sweet awe to take the body of their Lord, and Tomaso, who is priest's boy, tries not to look unduly puffed up by his office. After that you have dinner and a bottle of wine that ripened on the sunny slope of Escondito. All the week Father Shannon has shriven his people, who bring clean conscience to the betterment of appetite, and the Father sets them an example. Father Shannon is rather big about the middle to accommodate the large laugh that lives in him, but a most shrewd searcher of hearts. It is reported that one derives comfort from his confessional, and I for my part believe it.

The celebration of the Sixteenth, though it comes every year, takes as long to prepare for as Holy Communion. The señoritas have each a new dress apiece, the señoras a new *rebosa*. The young gentlemen have new silver trimmings to their sombreros, unspeakable ties, silk handkerchiefs, and new leathers to their spurs. At this time when the peppers glow in the gardens and the young quail cry "*cuidado*," "have a care!" you can hear the *plump, plump* of the *metate* from the alcoves of the vines where comfortable old dames, whose experience gives them the touch of art, are pounding out corn for tamales.

School-teachers from abroad have tried before now at Las Uvas to have school begin on the first of September, but got nothing else to stir in the heads of the little Castros, Garcias, and Romeros but feasts and cock-fights until after the Sixteenth. Perhaps you need to be told that this is the anniversary of the Republic, when liberty awoke and cried in the provinces of Old Mexico. You are aroused at midnight to hear them shouting in the streets, "*Vive la Libertad!*" answered from the houses and the recesses of the vines, "*Vive la Mexico!*" At sunrise shots are fired commemorating the tragedy of unhappy Maximilian, and then music, the noblest of national hymns, as the great flag of Old Mexico floats up the flag-pole in the bare little plaza of shabby Las Uvas. The sun over Pine Mountain greets the eagle of Montezuma before it touches the vineyards and the town, and the day begins with a great shout. By and by there will be a reading of the Declaration of Independence and an address punctured by *vives*; all the town in its best dress, and some exhibits of horsemanship that make lathered bits and bloodly spurs; also a cock-fight.

By night there will be dancing, and such music! old Santos to play the flute, a little lean man with a saintly countenance, young Garcia whose guitar has a soul, and Carrasco with the violin. They sit on a high platform above the dancers in the candle flare, backed by the red, white, and green of Old Mexico, and play fervently such music as you will not hear otherwise.

At midnight the flag comes down. Count yourself at a loss if you are not moved by that performance. Pine Mountain watches whitely overhead, shepherd fires glow strongly on the glooming hills. The plaza, the bare glistening pole, the dark folk, the bright dresses, are lit ruddily by a bonfire. It leaps up to the eagle flag, dies down, the music begins softly and aside. They play airs of old longing and exile; slowly out of the dark the flag drops down, bellying and falling with the midnight draught. Sometimes a hymn is sung, always there are tears. The flag is down; Tony Sevadra has received it in his arms. The music strikes a barbaric swelling tune, another flag begins a slow ascent,—it takes a breath or two to realize that they are both, flag and tune, the Star Spangled Banner,—a volley is fired, we are back, if you please, in California of America. Every youth who has the blood of patriots in him lays ahold on Tony Sevadra's flag, happiest if he can get a corner of it. The music goes before, the folk fall in two and two, singing. They sing everything, America, the Marseillaise, for the sake of the French shepherds hereabout, the hymn of Cuba, and the Chilian national air to comfort two families of that land. The flag goes to Doña Ina's, with the candlesticks and the altar cloths, then Las Uvas eats tamales and dances the sun up the slope of Pine Mountain.

You are not to suppose that they do not keep the Fourth,

Washington's Birthday, and Thanksgiving at the town of the grape vines. These make excellent occasions for quitting work and dancing, but the Sixteenth is the holiday of the heart. On Memorial Day the graves have garlands and new pictures of the saints tacked to the headboards. There is great virtue in an *Ave* said in the Camp of the Saints. I like that name which the Spanish speaking people give to the garden of the dead, *Campo Santo*, as if it might be some bed of healing from which blind souls and sinners rise up whole and praising God. Sometimes the speech of simple folk hints at truth the understanding does not reach. I am persuaded only a complex soul can get any good of a plain religion. Your earthborn is a poet and a symbolist. We breed in an environment of asphalt pavements a body of people whose creeds are chiefly restrictions against other people's way of life, and have kitchens and latrines under the same roof that houses their God. Such as these go to church to be edified, but at Las Uvas they go for pure worship and to entreat their God. The logical conclusion of the faith that every good gift cometh from God is the open hand and the finer courtesy. The meal done without buys a candle for the neighbor's dead child. You do foolishly to suppose that the candle does no good.

At Las Uvas every house is a piece of earth—thick walled, whitewashed adobe that keeps the even temperature of a cave; every man is an accomplished horseman and consequently bow-legged; every family keeps dogs, flea-bitten mongrels that loll on the earthen floors. They speak a purer Castilian than obtains in like villages of Mexico, and the way they count relationship everybody is more or less akin. There is not much villainy among them. What incentive to thieving or killing can there be when there is little wealth and that to be had for the borrowing! If they love too hotly, as we say "take their meat before grace," so do their betters. Eh, what! shall a man be a saint before he is dead? And besides, Holy Church takes it out of you one way or another before all is done. Come away, you who are obsessed with your own importance in the scheme of things, and have got nothing you did not sweat for, come away by the brown valleys and full-bosomed hills to the even-breathing days, to the kindliness, earthiness, ease of El Pueblo de Las Uvas.

from *The Flock*

Chapter III: A Shearing

To find a shearing, turn out from the towns of the southern San Joaquin at the time of the year when the hilltops begin to fray out in the multitudinous keen spears of the wild hyacinth, and look in the crumbling flakes of the foothill road for the tracks of the wool wagon. Here the roll of the valley up from the place of its lagoons is by long mesas breaking into summits and shoulders; successive crests of them reared up by slow, ample heavings, settling into folds, with long, valleyward slopes, and blunt mountain-facing heads, flung up at last in the sharp tumult of the Sierras. Thereward the trail of the wool wagon bears evenly and white. Over it, preceded by the smell of cigarettes, go the shearing crews of swarthy men with good manners and the air of opera pirates.

When Solomon Jewett held the ranch above the ford by the river which was Rio Bravo, and is now Kern, shearings went forward in a manner suited to the large leisure of the time. That was in the early sixties, when there were no laborers but Indians. These drove the flocks out in the shoulder-high grasses; "for in those days," said Jewett, "we never thought feed any good, less than eighteen inches high," and at the week end rounded them up at headquarters for the small allowance of whiskey that alone held them to the six days' job. It was a condition of the weekly dole that all knives and weapons should be first surrendered, but as you can imagine, whiskey being hard to come by at that time, much water went to each man's flask; the nearer the bottom of the cask the more water.

"*No werito*, Don Solomon, *no werito*," complained the herders as they saw the liquor paling in the flasks, but it was still worth such service as they rendered.

The ration at Rio Bravo was chiefly atole or "tole" of flour and water, coffee made thick with sugar, and raw mutton which every man cut off and toasted for himself; and a shearing then was a very jewel of the comfortable issue of labor. Of the day's allotment each man chose to shear what pleased him, and withdrawing, slept in the shade and the dust of the chaparral while his women struggled, with laughter and no bitterness of spirit, with the stubborn and over-wrinkled sheep. But even Indians, it seems, are amenable to the time, and I have it on the authority of Little Pete and the Manxman that Indians to-day make the best shearers, being crafty hand-workers and possessed of the communal instinct, liking to work and to loaf in company. Under the social stimulus they turn out an astonishing number of well-clipped muttons. Round the half moon of the lower San Joaquin the Mexicans are almost the only shearers to be had, and even the men who employ them credit them with the greatest fertility in excuses for quitting work.

All the lost weathers of romance collect between the ranges of the San Joaquin, like old galleons adrift in purple, open spaces of Sargasso. Shearing weather is a derelict from the time of Admetus; gladness comes out the earth and exhales light. It has its note, too, in pipings of the Dauphinoises, seated on the ground with gilias coming up between their knees while the flutes remember France. Under the low, false firmament of cloud, pools of luminosity collect in interlacing shallows of the hills. Here in one of those gentle swales where sheep were always meant to be, a ewe covers her belated lamb, or has stolen out from the wardship of the dogs to linger until the decaying clot of bones and hide, which was once her young, dissolves into its essences. The flock from which she strayed feeds toward the flutter of a white rag on the hilltop that signals a shearing going on in the clear space of a cañon below. Plain on the skyline with his sharp-eared dogs the herder leans upon his staff.

As many owners will combine for a shearing as can feed their flocks in the contiguous pastures. At Noriega's this year there were twenty-eight thousand head. Noriega's camp and corrals lie in the cañon of Poso Creek where there is a well of one burro power, for at this season the rains have not unlocked the sources of the stream. Hills march around it, shrubless, treeless; scarps of the Sierras stand up behind. Tents there are for stores, but all the operations of the camp are carried on out of doors. Confessedly or not, the several sorts of men who have to do with sheep mutually despise one another. Therefore the shearing crew has its own outfit, distinct from the camp of the hired herders.

Expect the best cooking and the worst smells at the camp of the French shepherds. It smells of mutton and old cheese, of onions and claret and garlic and tobacco, sustained and pervaded by the smell of sheep. This is the acceptable holiday smell, for when the far-called flocks come in to the shearing then is the only playtime the herder knows. Then if ever he gets a blink at a pretty girl, claret, and *bocie* at Vivian's, or a game of hand-ball at Noriega's, played with the great shovel-shaped gloves that are stamped with the name of Pamplona to remind him of home. But by the smell chiefly you should know something of the man whose camp you have come on unawares. When you can detect cheese at a dozen yards presume a Frenchman, but a leather wine bottle proves him a Basque, garlic and onions without cheese, a Mexican, and the absence of all these one of the variable types that calls itself American.

The shearing sheds face one side of the corrals and runways by which the sheep are passed through a chute to the shearers. The sheds, of which there may be a dozen, accommodate five or six shearers, and are, according to the notion of the owner, roofed and hung with canvas or lightly built of brush and blanket rags. Outside runs a shelf where the packers tie the wool. One of them stands at every shed with his tie-box and a hank of tie-cord wound about his body. This tie-box is merely a wooden frame of the capacity of one fleece, notched to hold the cord, which, once adjusted, can be tightened with a jerk and a hitch or two, making the fleece into a neat, square bundle weighing six to ten pounds as the clip runs light or heavy. Besides these, there must go to a full shearing crew two men to handle the wool sacks and one to sit on the packed fleeces and keep tally as the shearer cries his own number and the number of his sheep, betraying his country by his tongue.

"*Numero neuf, onze!*" sings the shearer.

"*Numero neuf, onze!*" drones the marker.

"*Cinco; viente!*"

"*Numero cinco; viente!* tally."

I have heard Little Pete keep tally in three languages at once.

The day's work begins stiffly, little laughter, and the leisurely whet of shears. The pulse of work rises with the warmth, the crisp bite of the blades, the rustle and scamper of sheep in the corral beat into rhythm with the bent backs rising and stooping to the incessant cry, "*Numero diez, triente!*" "Number ten, tally!" closing full at noon with the clink of canteens. Afternoon sees the sweat dripping and a freer accompaniment of talk, drowned again in the rising fever of work at the turn of the day, after which the smell of cooking begins to climb above the smells of the corrals. A man wipes his shears on his overalls and hangs them up when he has clipped the forty or fifty sheep that his wage, necessity, or his reputation demands of him.

Two men can sack the wool of a thousand sheep in a day, though their contrivances are the simplest,—a frame tall enough to be taller than a wool sack, which is once and a half as tall as Little Pete, an iron ring over which the wetted mouth of the sack is turned and so held fast to the top of the frame, a pole to support the weight of the sack while the packer sews it up. Once the sack is adjusted with ears tied in the bottom corners over a handful of wool, the bundled fleeces are tossed up into it and trampled close by the packer as the sack fills and fills. The pole works under the frame like an ancient wellsweep, hoisting the three hundred pound weight of wool while the packer closes the top.

For the reason why wool shears are ground dull at the point, and for knowing about the yolk of the wool, I commend you to Noriega or Little Pete; this much of a shearing is their business; the rest of it is romance and my province.

The far-called flocks come in; Raymundo has climbed to the top of the wool sack tower and spies for the dust of their coming; dust in the east against the roan-colored hills; dust in the misty, blue ring of the west; high dust under Breckenridge floating across the banked poppy fires; flocks moving on the cactus-grown mesa. Now they wheel, and the sun shows them white and newly shorn; there passes the band of Jean Moynier, shorn yesterday. Northward the sagebrush melts and stirs in a stream of moving shadow.

"That," says Raymundo, "should be Étienne Picquard; when he

goes, he goes fast; when he rests, he rests altogether. Now he shall pay me for that crook he had of me last year."

"Look over against the spotted hill, there by the white scar," says a little red man who has just come in. "See you anything?"

"Buzzards flying over," says Raymundo from the sacking frame.

"By noon, then, you should see a flock coming; it should be White Mountain Joe. I passed him Tuesday. He has a cougar's skin, the largest ever. Four nights it came, and on the fourth it stayed."

So announced and forerun by word of their adventures the herders of the Long Trail come in. At night, like kinsmen met in hostelries, they talk between spread pallets by the dying fires.

"You, Octavieu, you think you are the only one who has the ill fortune, you and your poisoned meadows! When I came by Oak Creek I lost twoscore of my lambs to the forest ranger. Twoscore fat and well grown. We fed along the line of the Reserve, and the flock scattered. Ah, how should I know, there being no monuments at that place! They went but a flock length over, that I swear to you, and the ranger came riding on us from the oaks and charged the sheep; he was a new man and a fool not to know that a broken flock travels up. The more he ran after them the farther they went in the Reserve. Twoscore lambs were lost in the steep rocks, or died from the running, and of the ewes that lost their lambs seven broke back in the night, and I could not go in to the Reserve to hunt them. And how is that for ill fortune? You with your halfscore of scabby wethers!"

Trouble with forest rangers is a fruitful topic, and brings a stream of invective that falls away as does all talk out of doors to a note of humorous large content. Jules upbraids his collie tenderly:—

"So you would run away to the town, eh, and get a beating for your pains; you are well served, you misbegotten son of a thief! Know you not there is none but old Jules can abide the sight of you?"

Echenique by the fire is beginning a bear story:—

"It was four of the sun when he came upon me where I camped by the Red Hill northward from Agua Hedionda and would have taken my best wether, Duroc, that I have raised by my own hand.

I, being a fool, had left my gun at Tres Pinos on account of the rangers. Eh, I would not have cared for a sheep more or less, but Duroc!—when I think of that I go at him with my staff, for I am seven times a fool, and the bear he leaves the sheep to come after me. Well I know the ways of bears, that they can run faster than a man up a hill or down; but around and around, that is where the great weight of Monsieur le Bear has him at fault. So long as you run with the side of the hill the bear comes out below you. Now this Red Hill where I am camped is small, that a man might run around it in half an hour. So I run and the bear runs; when I come out again by my sheep I speak to the dogs that they keep them close. Then I run around and around, and this second time—Sacre!"

He gets upon his feet as there rises a sudden scurry from the flock, turned out that evening from the shearing pens and bedded on the mesa's edge, yearning toward the fresh feed. Echenique lifts up his staff and whistles to his dogs; like enough the flock will move out in the night to feed and the herder with him. Not until they meet again by chance, in the summer meadows, will each and several hear the end of the bear story. So they recount the year's work by the shearing fires, and if they be hirelings of different owners, lie to each other about the feed. Dogs snuggle to their masters; for my part I believe they would take part in the conversation if they could, and suffer in the deprivation.

At shearings flocks are reorganized for the Long Trail. Wethers and non-productive ewes are cut out for market, yearlings change hands, lambs are marked, herders outfitted. The shearing crew which has begun in the extreme southern end of the valley passes north on the trail of vanishing snows as far as Montana, and picks up the fall shearings, rounding toward home. This is a recent procedure. Once there was time enough for a *fiesta* lasting two or three days, or at the least a shearing *baile*. I remember very well when at Adobe, before the wind had cleared the litter of fleeces, they would be riding at the ring and clinking the shearing wage over cockfights and monte. Toward nightfall from somewhere in the blue-and-white desertness, music of guitars floated in the prettiest girls in the company of limber vaqueros, clinking their spurs and shaking from their hair the shining crease where the heavy sombrero had rested. Middle-aged señoras wound their fat arms in their rebosas and sat against the wall; blue smoke of cigarettes began to sway with the strum of the plucked guitar; cascarones would fly about, breaking in bright tinsel showers. O, the sound of the mandolin, and the rose in the señorita's hair! *What* is it in the Castilian strain that makes it possible for a girl to stick a rose behind her ear and cause you to forget the smell of garlic and the reek of unwashed walls?

Along about the middle hours, heaves up, heralded by soft clink-ings, and girding of broad tires, the freighter's twenty-eight-mule team. The teamsters, who have pushed their fagged animals miles beyond their daily stunt to this end, drop the reins to the swamper and whirl with undaunted freshness to the dance. As late as seven o'clock in the morning you could still see their ruddy or freckled faces glowing above the soft, dark heads. Though if you had sheep in charge you could hardly have stayed so long. Outside so far that the light that rays from the crevices of the bursting doors of Adobe is no brighter than his dying fire, the herder lies with his sheep, and by the time the bleached hollows of the sands collect shadows ten-uous and blue, has begun to move his flock toward the much desired Sierra pastures.

from *Chapter VI: The Open Range*

All the winds of its open places smell of sage, and all its young rivers are swift. They begin thin and crystalline from under the forty-foot drifts, grow thick and brown in the hot leaps of early summer, run clear with full throaty laughter in midseason, froth and cloud to quick, far-off rains, fall off to low and golden-mottled rills before the first of the snows. By their changes the herder camped a hundred miles from his summer pastures knows what goes forward in them.

Let me tell you this,—every sort of life has its own zest for those who are bred to it. No more delighted sense of competency and power goes to the man who from his wire web controls the movement of money and wheat, than to the shepherd who by the passage of birds, by the stream tones, by the drift of pine pollen on the eddies of slack water, keeps tally of the pastures. Do you read the notes of mountain color as they draw into dusk? There is a color of blue, deeply pure as a trumpet tone low in the scale, that announces rain there is a hot blue mist suffusing into gold as it climbs against the horizon, that promises wind. There is a sense that wakes in the night with a warning to keep the flock close, and another sense of the shortest direction. The smell of the sheep is to the herder as the smack and savor of any man's work. Also it is possible to felicitate one's self on rounding a feeding flock and bringing it to a standstill within a flock-length.

The whole of that great country northward is so open and well-ordered that it affords the freest exercise of shepherd craft, every man going about to seek the preferred pastures for which use has bred a liking. Miles and miles of that district are dusky white with sage, falling off to cienagas,—grassy hollows of seeping springs,—cooled by the windy flood that sets from the mountain about an hour before noon. The voice of that country is an open whisper, pointed at intervals by the deep whir-r-r-r of the sage hens rising from some place of hidden waters. Times when there is moonlight, watery and cold, a long thin howl detaches itself from any throat and welters on the wind....

The sagebrush grows up to an elevation of eight or nine thousand feet and the wind has not quite lapped up the long-backed drifts from its hollows when the sheep come in. A month later there will begin to be excellent browse along the lower pine borders, meadow sweet, buckthorns, and sulphur flower. The yellow pines, beaten by the wind, or at the mere stir of pine warblers and grosbeaks in their branches, give out clouds of pollen dust.

The suffusion of light over the Sierra highlands is singular. Broad bands of atmosphere infiltrating the minareted crests seem not to be penetrated by it, but the sage, the rounded backs of the sheep, the clicking needles of the pines give it back in luminous particles infinitely divided. Airy floods of it pour about the plats of white and purple heather and deepen vaporously blue at the bases of the headlands. Long shafts of it at evening fall so obliquely as to strike far under the ragged bellies of the sheep. Wind approaches from the high places; even at the highest it drops down from unimagined steeps of air. When it moves in a cañon, before ever the near torches of the castilleia are stirred by it, far up you hear the crescendo tone of the fretted waters, first as it were the foam of sound blown toward you, and under it the pounding of the falls. Then it runs with a patter in the quaking asp; now it takes a fir and wrestles with it; it wakes the brushwood with a whistle; in the soft dark of night it tugs at the corners of the bed.

Weather warnings in a hill country are short but unmistakable; it is not well anywhere about the Sierras to leave the camp uncovered if one must move out of reach of it. And if the herder tires of precautions let him go eastward of the granite ranges where there is no weather. Let him go by the Hot Creek country, by Dead Man's Gulch and the Sucking Sands, by the lava flats and the pink and roan-colored hills where the lost mines are, by the black hills of pellucid glass where the sage gives place to the bitter brush, the *wheno-nabe* where the carrion crows catch grasshoppers and the coyotes eat juniper berries, where, during the months man finds it possible to stay in them, there is no weather. Let him go, if he can stand it, where the land is naked and not ashamed, where it is always shut night or wide-open day with no interval but the pinkish violet hour of the alpen glow. There is forage enough in good years and water if you know where to look for it. Indians resorted there once to gather winter stores from the grey nut-pines that head out roundly on the eight thousand foot levels each in its clear wide space. The sand between them is strewn evenly with charred flakes of roasted cones and the stone circles about the pits are powdered still with ashes, for, as I have said, there is no weather there.

There are some pleasant places in this district, nice and trivial as the childhood reminiscences of senility, but the great laps and folds of the cañons are like the corrugations in the faces of the indecently aged. There is a look about men who come from sojourning in that country as if the sheer nakedness of the land had somehow driven the soul back on its elemental impulses. You can imagine that one type of man exposed to it would become a mystic and another incredibly brutalized.

The devotion of the herder to the necessities of the flock is become a proverb. In a matter of urgent grazing these hairy little Bascos would feed their flocks to the rim of the world and a little over it, but I think they like best to stay where the days and nights are not all of one piece, where after the flare of the storm-trumpeting sunsets, they can snuggle to the blankets and hear the rain begin to drum on the canvas covers, and mornings see the shudder of the flock under the lift of the cloud-mist like the yellowing droves of breakers in a fog backing away from the ferries in the bay. Pleasant it is also in the high valleys where the pines begin, to happen on friendly camps of Indians come up in clans and families to gather larvae of pine borers, *chia*, ground cherries, and sunflower seed. One could well leave the flock with the dogs for an hour to see the firelight redden on carefree faces and hear the soft laughter of the women, bubbling as hidden water in the dark.

***

It was not until most of the things I have been writing to you about had happened; after Narcisse Duplin had died because of Suzon Moynier, and Suzon had died; after the two Lausannes had found each other and Finot had won a fortune in a lottery and gone back to France to spend it; but not long after the wavering of the tariff and its final adjustment had brought the sheep business to its present status, that the flocks began to be tabooed of the natural forest lands.

One must think of the coniferous belt of the Sierra Nevadas as it appears from the top of the tremendous uplift about the head of Kern and Kings rivers, as a dark mantle laid over the range, rent sharply by the dove-grey sierra, conforming to the large contours of the mountains and fraying raggedly along the cañons; a sombre cloak to the mysteries by which the drainage of this watershed is made into live rivers.

Above the pines rears a choppy and disordered surf of stone, lakes in its hollows of the clear jade that welters below the shoreward lift of waves. From the troughs of the upflung peaks the shining drifts sag back. By the time they have shortened so much that the honey flutes of the wild columbine call the bees to the upper limit of trees, the flocks have melted into the wood. They feed on the chaparral up from the stream borders and in the hanging meadows that are freed first from the flood of snow-water; the raking hoofs sink deeply in the damp, loosened soil. As the waste of the drifts gathers into runnels they follow it into filled lake basins and cut off the hope of a thousand blossomy things. Then they begin to seek out the hidden meadows, deep wells of pleasantness that the pines avoid because of wetness, soddy and good and laced by bright waters, Manache meadows girdling the red hills, Kearsarge meadows above the white-barked pines, Big meadows where the creek goes smoothly on the glacier slips, Short-Hair meadows, Tehippeti meadows under the dome where the haunted water has a sound of bells, meadows of the Twin Lakes and Middle-Fork, meadows of Yosemite, of Stinking Water, and Angustora.

Chains of meadows there are that lie along creek borders, new meadows at the foot of steep snow-shedding cliffs, shut pastures flock-journeys apart, where no streams run out and no trails lead in, and between them over the connecting moraines, over the dividing knife-blade ridges go the pines in open order with the young hope of the forest coming up under them. No doubt meadow grasses, all plants that renew from the root, were meant for forage, and for getting at them wild grazing beasts were made fleet. But nothing other than fear puts speed in man-herded flocks. Seed-renewing plants come up between the tree boles, tufty grass, fireweed, shinleaf, and pipsisiwa; these the slow-moving flocks must crop, and unavoidably along with them the seedling pines; then as by successive croppings, forest floors are cleared, they nip the tender ends of young saplings, for the business of the flock is to feed and to keep on feeding. Where the forest intervals afforded no more grazing, good shepherds set them alight and looked for new pastures to spring up in the burned districts. Who knew how far the fire crept in the brown litter or heard it shrieking as it ran up the tall masts of pines, or saw the wild supplications of its pitchy smoke? As for the shepherd, he fed forward with the flocks over the shrubby moraines. When the thick chaparral made difficult passage, when it tore the wool, the good shepherd set the fire to rip out a path, and the next year found tender, sappy browze springing from the undying roots. The flock came to the meadows; they fed close; then the foreplanning herder turned the creek from its course to water it anew and the rainbow trout died gasping on the sod.

I say the good shepherd—the man who makes good the destiny of flocks to bear wool and produce mutton. For what else fares he forth with his staff and his dogs? A shepherd is not a forester, nor is he the only sort of man ignorant and scornful of the advantage of covered watersheds. When he first went about the business of putting the mountain to account, the greatest number to whom water for irrigation is the greatest good had not arrived. If in the seventies and eighties here and there a sheepman had arisen to declare for the Forest Reserve, who of the Powers would have heard him, which of the New Englanders who are now orange-growers would have understood his speech? In fact many did so deliver themselves. The unrestricted devotion of the pine belt to the sheep has done us damage; but let us say no more about it lest we be made ashamed.

from *Chapter VII: The Flock*

The earliest important achievement of ovine intelligence is to know whether its own notion or another's is most worth while, and if the other's, which one. Individual sheep have certain qualities, instincts, competencies, but in the man-herded flocks these are superseded by something which I shall call the flock-mind, though I cannot say very well what it is, except that it is less than the sum of all their intelligences. This is why there have never been any notable changes in the management of flocks since the first herder girt himself with a wallet of sheepskin and went out of his cave dwelling to the pastures.

Understand that a flock is not the same thing as a number of sheep. On the stark wild headlands of the White Mountains, as many as thirty Bighorn are known to run in loose, fluctuating hordes; in fenced pastures, two to three hundred; close-herded on the range, two to three thousand; but however artificially augmented, the flock is always a conscious adjustment. As it is made up in the beginning of the season, the band is chiefly of one sort, wethers or ewes or weanling lambs (for the rams do not run with the flock except for a brief season in August); with a few flockwise ones, trained goats, the *cabestres* of the Mexican herders, trusted bell-wethers or experienced old ewes mixed and intermeddled by the herder and the dogs, becoming invariably and finally coordinate. There are always Leaders, Middlers, and Tailers, each insisting on its own place in the order of going. Should the flock be rounded up suddenly in alarm it mills within itself until these have come to their own places.

If you would know something of the temper and politics of the shepherd you meet, inquire of him for the names of his leaders. They should be named for his sweethearts, for the little towns of France, for the generals of the great Napoleon, for the presidents of Republics,—though for that matter they are all ardent republicans, —for the popular heroes of the hour. Good shepherds take the greatest pains with their leaders, not passing them with the first flock to slaughter, but saving them to make wise the next.

There is much debate between herders as to the advantage of goats over sheep as leaders. In any case there are always a few goats in a flock, and most American owners prefer them; but the Frenchmen choose bell-wethers. Goats lead naturally by reason of a quicker instinct, forage more freely, and can find water on their own account. But wethers, if trained with care, learn what goats abhor, to take broken ground sedately, to walk through the water rather than set the whole flock leaping and scrambling; but never to give voice to alarm as goats will, and call the herder. Wethers are more bidable once they are broken to it, but a goat is the better for a good beating. Echenique has told me that the more a goat com- plains under his cudgelings the surer he is of the brute's need of dis- cipline. Goats afford another service in furnishing milk for the shepherd, and, their udders being most public, will suckle a sick lamb, a pup, or a young burro at need.

It appears that leaders understand their office, and goats particu- larly exhibit a jealousy of their rights to be first over the stepping- stones or to walk the teetering log-bridges at the roaring creeks. By this facile reference of the initiative to the wisest one, the shepherd is served most. The dogs learn to which of the flock to communicate orders, at which heels a bark or a bite soonest sets the flock in motion. But the flock-mind obsesses equally the best trained, flashes as instantly from the Meanest of the Flock.

Suppose the sheep to scatter widely on a heather-planted head- land, the leader feeding far to windward. Comes a cougar sneaking up the trail between the rooted boulders toward the Meanest of the Flock. The smell of him, the play of light on his sleek flanks startles the unslumbering fear in the Meanest; it runs widening in the flock-mind, exploding instantly in the impulse of flight.

Danger! flashes the flock-mind, and in danger the indispensable thing is to run, not to wait until the leader sniffs the tainted wind and signals it; not for each and singly to put the occasion to the proof; but to run—of this the flock-mind apprises—and to keep on running until the impulse dies faintly as water-rings on the surface of a mantling pond. In the wild pastures flight is the only succor, and since to cry out is to interfere with that business and draw on the calamity, a flock in extremity never cries out.

Consider, then, the inadequacy of the flock-mind. A hand-fed leader may learn to call the herder vociferously, a cosset lamb in trouble come blatting to his heels, but the flock has no voice other than the deep-mouthed pealings hung about the leader's neck. In all that darkling lapse of time since herders began to sleep by the sheep with their weapons, affording a protection that the flock-mind never learns to invite, they have found no better trick than to be still and run foolishly. For the flock-mind moves only in the direction of the Original Intention. When at shearings or markings they run the yearlings through a gate for counting, the rate of going accelerates until the sheep pass too rapidly for numbering. Then the shepherd thrusts his staff across the opening, forcing the next sheep to jump, and the next, and the next, until, Jump! says the flock-mind. Then he withdraws the staff, and the sheep go on jumping until the impulse dies as the dying peal of the bells.

By very little the herder may turn the flock-mind to his advantage, but chiefly it works against him. Suppose on the open range the impulse to forward movement overtakes them, set in motion by some eager leaders that remember enough of what lies ahead to make them oblivious to what they pass. They press ahead. The flock draws on. The momentum of travel grows. The bells clang soft and hurriedly; the sheep forget to feed; they neglect the tender pastures; they will not stay to drink. Under an unwise or indolent herder the sheep going on an accustomed trail will over-travel and under-feed, until in the midst of good pasture they starve upon their feet. So it is on the Long Trail you so often see the herder walking with his dogs ahead of his sheep to hold them back to feed. But if it should be new ground he must go after and press them skillfully, for the flock-mind balks chiefly at the unknown.

If a flock could be stopped as suddenly as it is set in motion, Sanger would never have lost to a single bear the five hundred sheep he told me of. They were bedded on a mesa breaking off in a precipice two hundred feet above the valley, and the bear came up behind them in the moonless watch of night. With no sound but the scurry of feet and the startled clamor of the bells, the flock broke straight ahead. The brute instinct had warned them asleep but it could not save them awake. All that the flock-mind could do was to stir them instantly to running, and they fled straight away over the headland, piling up, five hundred of them, in the gulch below.

In sudden attacks from several quarters, or inexplicable man-thwarting of their instincts, the flock-mind teaches them to turn a solid front, revolving about in the smallest compass with the lambs in the midst, narrowing and in-drawing until they perish by suffocation. So they did in the intricate defiles of Red Rock, where Carrier lost two hundred and fifty in '74, and at Poison Springs, as Narcisse Duplin told me, where he had to choose between leaving them to the deadly waters, or, prevented from the spring, made witless by thirst, to mill about until they piled up and killed threescore in their midst. By no urgency of the dogs could they be moved forward or scattered until night fell with coolness and returning sanity. Nor does the imperfect gregariousness of man always save us from ill-considered rushes or strangulous in-turnings of the social mass. Notwithstanding there are those who would have us to be flock-minded.

It is probable that the obsession of this over-sense originates in the extraordinary quickness with which the sheep makes the superior intelligence of the leader serve his own end. A very little running in the open range proves that one in every group of sheep has sharper vision, quicker hearing, keener scent; henceforth it is the business of the dull sheep to watch that favored one. No slightest sniff or stamp escapes him; the order for flight finds him with muscles tense for running.

The worth of a leader in close-herded flocks is his ability to catch readily the will of the herder. Times I have seen the sheep feeding far from the man, not knowing their appointed bedding-place. The dogs lag at the herder's heels. Now as the sun is going down the man thrusts out his arm with a gesture that conveys to the dogs his wish that they turn the flock toward a certain open scarp. The dogs trot out leisurely, circling widely to bring up the farthest stragglers, but before they round upon it the flock turns. It moves toward the appointed quarter and pours smoothly up the hill. It is possible that the leaders may have learned the language of that right arm, and in times of quietude obey it without intervention of the dogs. It is also conceivable that in the clear silences of the untroubled wild the flock-mind takes its impulse directly from the will of the herder.

* * *

Almost the only sense left untouched by man-herding is the weather sense. Scenting a change, the sheep exhibit a tendency to move to higher ground; no herder succeeds in making his flock feed in the eye of the sun. While rain falls they will not feed nor travel except in extreme desperation, but if after long falling it leaves off suddenly, night or day, the flock begins to crop. Then if the herder hears not the bells nor wakes himself by that subtle sense which in the outdoor life has time to grow, he has his day's work cut out for him in the rounding-up. A season of long rains makes short fleeces.

Summers in the mountains, sheep love to lie on the cooling banks and lick the snow, preferring it to any drink; but if falling snow overtakes them they are bewildered by it, find no food for themselves, and refuse to travel while it lies on the ground. This is the more singular, for the American wild sheep, the Bighorn, makes nothing of a twenty foot fall; in the blinding swirl of flakes shifts only to let the drifts pile under him; ruminates most contentedly when the world is full of a roaring white wind. Most beasts in bad weather drift before a storm. The faster it moves the farther go the sheep; so if there arises one of those blowy days that announce the turn of the two seasons, blinding thick with small dust, at the end of a few hours of it the shepherd sees the tails of his sheep disappearing down the wind. The tendency of sheep is to seek lower ground when disturbed by beasts, and under weather stress to work up. When any of his flock are strayed or stampeded, the herder knows by the occasion whether to seek them up hill or down. Seek them he must if he would have them again, for strays have no faculty by sense or scent to work their way back to the herd. Let them be separated from it but by the roll of the land, and by accident headed in another direction, it is for them as if the flock had never been. It is to provide against this incompetency that the shepherd makes himself markers, a black sheep, or one with a crumpled horn or an unshorn patch on the rump, easily noticeable in the shuffle of dust-colored backs. It is the custom to have one marker to one hundred sheep, each known by his chosen place in the flock which he insists upon, so that if as many as half a dozen stray out of the band the relative position of the markers is changed; or if one of these conspicuous ones be missing it will not be singly, because of the tendency of large flocks to form smaller groups about the best worth following.

from *Chapter IX: The Strife of the Herdsmen*

The mesa was blue with the little blue larkspur the Indians love; a larkspur sky began somewhere infinitely beyond the Sierra wall and stretched far and faintly over Shoshone Land. The ring of the horizon was as blue as the smoke of the deputy sheriff's cigar as he lay in the shade of a boulder and guessed almost by the manner of the dust how many and what brands stirred up the visible warning of their approach. The spring passage of the flocks had begun, and we were out after the tax.

Two banners of dust went up in the gaps of the Alabamas and one below the point, two at Symmes Creek, one crowded up under Williamson, one by the new line of willows below Piñon, that by the time the shadows of the mountains had shrunk into their crevices, proved by the sound of the bells to be the flock of Narcisse Duplin. The bell of Narcisse's best leader, Le Petit Corporal, was notable; large as a goat-skin wine-bottle, narrowing at the mouth, and so long that it scraped the sand when the Corporal browsed on the bitter brush and lay quite along the ground when he cropped the grass. The sound of it struck deeply under all the notes of the day, and carried as far as the noise of the water pouring into the pot-hole below Kearsarge Mill.

The deputy sheriff had finished his cigar, and begun telling me about Manuel de Borba after he had killed Mariana in the open below Olancha. Naylor and Robinson bought the flock of him in good faith, though suspicion began to grow in them as they came

north with it toward the place where Mariana lived; then it spread
in Lone Pine until it became a rumor and finally a conviction.
Then Relles Carrasco took up the back trail and found, at the end
of it, Mariana lying out in the sage, full of knife wounds, and the
wounds were in his back. When the deputy had proceeded as far as
the search for de Borba, Narcisse came up with us.

Where we sat the wash of Pine Creek was shallow, and below lay
the rude, tottering bridge of sticks and stones, such as sheepmen
build everywhere in the Sierras for getting sheep across trouble-
some streams. Here in the course of the day came all the flocks we
sighted, with others drifting into view in the south, and at twilight
tide a dozen of their fires blossomed under Kearsarge in the dusk.
The sheriff counted the sheep as they went singly over the bridge,
with his eyes half shut against the sun and his finger wagging; as
for me, I went up and down among the larkspur flowers, among the
lupines and the shining bubbles of mariposa floating along the tops
of the scrub, and renewed acquaintance.

"Tell me," I said to Narcisse, who because of the tawny red of his
hair, the fiery red of his face, the russet red of his beard, and the red
spark of his eye, was called Narcisse the Red, "tell me what is the
worst of shepherding?"

"The worst, madame, is the feed, because there is not enough of it."

"And what, in your thinking, is the best?"

"The feed, madame, for there is not enough of it."

"But how could that be, both best and worst?"

Narcisse laughed full and throatily, throwing up his chin from
the burned red chest all open to the sun. It was that laugh of
Narcisse's that betrayed him the night he carried away Suzon
Moynier from her father's house.

"It is the worst," said he, "because it is a great distress to see the
flock go hungry, also it is a loss to the owner. It is the best, because
every man must set his wits against every other. When he comes
out of the hills with a fat flock and good fleeces it is that he has
proved himself the better man. He knows the country better and
has the greater skill to keep other men from his pastures. How else
but by contriving shall a man get the feed from the free pastures
when it goes every year to the best contriver? You think you would
not do it? Suppose now you have come with a lean flock to good

ground sufficient for yours only, and before the sheep have had a fill of it, comes another blatting band working against the wind. You walk to and fro behind your flock, you take out a newspaper to read, you unfold it. Suddenly the wind takes it from your hand, carries it rustling white and fearsome in the faces of the approaching flock. Ah, bah! Who would have supposed they would stampede for so slight a thing? And by the time their herder has rounded them up, your sheep will have all the feed."

When Narcisse Duplin tells me this the eyes of all the herders twinkle; glints of amusement run from one to another like white hints of motion in the water below the birches.

"It is so," said Octavieu, the blue-eyed Basque, "the feed is his who can keep it. Madame goes much about the Sierras, have you not seen the false monuments?"

"And been misled by them."

"They were not meant for such as madame, but one shepherd when he finds a good meadow makes a false trail leading around and away from it, and another shepherd coming is deceived thereby, and the meadow is kept secret for the finder."

When Octavieu tells me this I recall a story I have heard of Little Pete, how when he had turned his flocks into an upper meadow he met a herder bound to that same feeding-ground, and by a shorter route; but the day saved him. No matter how much they neglect the calendar, French shepherds always know when it is the fourteenth of July, as if they had a sense for divining it much as gophers know when *taboose* is good to eat. Pete dug up a bottle from his cayaques.

"*Allons, mon vieux, c'est le quatorze Juillet*," cried the strategist; "come, a toast; *Le Quatorze Juillet!*"

"*Le Quatorze Juillet!*"

The red liquor gurgled in their throats. Never yet was a Frenchman proof against patriotism and wine and good company. The arrested flock shuffled and sighed while Pete and their master through the rosy glow of wine saw the Bastile come down and the Tricolor go up. Incidentally they saw also the bottom of the bottle, and by that time Pete's flock was in full possession of the meadow. Pete laughs at this story and denies it, but so light-heartedly that I am sure that if it never happened it was because he happened never to think of it.

"However, I will tell you a true story," said he. "I was once in a country where there was a meadow with springs and much good feed in that neighborhood, but unwatered, so that if a man had not the use of the meadow he could get no good of it. The place where the spring was, being patented land, belonged to a man whose name does not come into the story. I write to that man and make him a price for the water and the feed, but the answer is not come. Still I think sure to have it, and leave word that the letter is to be sent to me at the camp, and move my flock every day toward the meadow. Also I observe another sheepman feeding about my trail, and I wish greatly for that letter, for I think he makes the eyes at that pasture with springs.

"All this would be no matter if I could trust my herder, but I have seen him sit by the other man's fire, and I know that he has what you call the grudge against me. For what? How should I know? Maybe there is not garlic enough in camp, maybe I keep the wine too close; and it is written in the foreheads of some men that they should be false to their employers. When it is the better part of a week gone I am sure that my herder has told the other man that I have not yet rented the springs, so I resolve at night in my blanket what I shall do. That day I send out my man with his part of the sheep very far, then I write me a letter, to me, Pierre Giraud, and put it in the camp. It is stamped, and altogether such as if it had come from the Post Office. Then I ride about my business for the day, and at night when I come late to the camp there is the herder who sings out to me and says:—

"'Here is your letter come.'"

Pete chuckles inwardly with true artistic appreciation of finesse. "Eh, if you do this sort of thing it should be done thoroughly. I see the herder watch me with the tail of his eye while I make to read the letter.

"'Is it right about the meadow?' says he.

"'You can see,' say I, and I hand him the paper, which he cannot read, but he will not confess to that. That night he goes to the other man's fire, and the next day I see that that one drops off from my trail, and I know he has had word of my letter. Then I move my sheep up to the meadow of springs."

"And the real letter, when it came—if it came?"

"That you should ask me!" cries Pete, and I am not sure if I am the more convinced by the reproachful waggings of his head or the deep, delighted twinkle of his eye.

from *The California Earthquake of 1906*

EDITED BY DAVID STARR JORDAN

The Temblor

There are some fortunes harder to bear once they are done with than while they are doing, and there are three things that I shall never be able to abide in quietness again—the smell of burning, the creaking of house-beams in the night, and the roar of a great city going past me in the street.

Ours was a quiet neighborhood in the best times; undisturbed except by the hawker's cry or the seldom whistling hum of the wire, and in the two days following April eighteenth, it became a little lane out of Destruction. The first thing I was aware of was being wakened sharply to see my bureau lunging solemnly at me across the width of the room. It got up first on one castor and then on another, like the table at a séance, and wagged its top portentously. It was an antique pattern, tall and marble-topped, and quite heavy enough to seem for the moment sufficient cause for all the uproar. Then I remember standing in the doorway to see the great barred leaves of the entrance on the second floor part quietly as under an unseen hand, and beyond them, in the morning grayness, the rose tree and the palms replacing one another, as in a moving picture, and suddenly an eruption of night-gowned figures crying out that it was only an earthquake, but I had already made this discovery for myself as I recall trying to explain. Nobody having suffered much in our immediate vicinity, we were left free to perceive that the very instant after the quake was tempered by the half-humorous, wholly American appreciation of a thoroughly good job. Half an hour after the temblor people sitting on their doorsteps, in bathrobes and kimonos, were admitting to each other with a half twist of laughter between tremblings that it was a really creditable shake.

The appreciation of calamity widened slowly as water rays on a mantling pond. Mercifully the temblor came at an hour when families had not divided for the day, but live wires sagging across housetops were to outdo the damage of falling walls. Almost before the dust of ruined walls had ceased rising, smoke began to go up against the sun, which, by nine of the clock, showed bloodshot through it as the eye of Disaster.

It is perfectly safe to believe anything any one tells you of personal adventure; the inventive faculty does not exist which could outdo the actuality; little things prick themselves on the attention as the index of the greater horror.

I remember distinctly that in the first considered interval after the temblor, I went about and took all the flowers out of the vases to save the water that was left; and that I went longer without washing my face than I ever expect to again.

I recall the red flare of a potted geranium undisturbed on a window ledge in a wall of which the brickwork dropped outward, while the roof had gone through the flooring; and the cross-section of a lodging house parted cleanly with all the little rooms unaltered, and the halls like burrows, as if it were the home of some superior sort of insect laid open to the microscope.

South of Market, in the district known as the Mission, there were cheap man-traps folded in like pasteboard, and from these, before the rip of the flames blotted out the sound, arose the thin, long scream of mortal agony.

Down on Market Street Wednesday morning, when the smoke from the burning blocks behind began to pour through the windows we saw an Italian woman kneeling on the street corner praying quietly. Her cheap belongings were scattered beside her on the ground and the crowd trampled them; a child lay on a heap of clothes and bedding beside her, covered and very quiet. The woman opened her eyes now and then, looked at the reddening smoke and addressed herself to prayer as one sure of the stroke of fate. It was not until several days later that it occurred to me why the baby lay so quiet, and why the woman prayed instead of flying.

Not far from there, a day-old bride waited while her husband went back to the ruined hotel for some papers he had left, and the cornice fell on him; then a man who had known him, but not that he was married, came by and carried away the body and shipped it out of the city, so that for four days the bride knew not what had become of him.

There was a young man who, seeing a broken and dismantled grocery, meant no more than to save some food, for already the certainty of famine was upon the city—and was shot for looting. Then his women came and carried the body away, mother and betrothed, and laid it on the grass until space could be found for burial. They drew a handkerchief over its face, and sat quietly beside it without bitterness or weeping. It was all like this, broken bits of human tragedy, curiously unrelated, inconsequential, disrupted by the temblor, impossible to this day to gather up and compose into a proper picture.

The largeness of the event had the effect of reducing private sorrow to a mere pin prick and a point of time. Everybody tells you tales like this with more or less detail. It was reported that two blocks from us a man lay all day with a placard on his breast that he was shot for looting, and no one denied the aptness of the warning. The will of the people was toward authority, and everywhere the tread of soldiery brought a relieved sense of things orderly and secure. It was not as if the city had waited for martial law to be declared, but as if it precipitated itself into that state by instinct as its best refuge.

In the parks were the refugees huddled on the damp sod with insufficient bedding and less food and no water. They laughed. They had come out of their homes with scant possessions, often the least serviceable. They had lost business and clientage and tools, and they did not know if their friends had fared worse. Hot, stifling smoke billowed down upon them, cinders pattered like hail—and they laughed—not hysteria, but the laughter of unbroken courage.

That exodus to the park did not begin in our neighborhood until the second day; all the first day was spent in seeing such things as I relate, while confidently expecting the wind to blow the fire another way. Safe to say one-half the loss of household goods might have been averted, had not the residents been too sure of such exemption. It happened not infrequently that when a man had seen his women safe he went out to relief work and returning found smoking ashes—and the family had left no address. We were told of those who had dead in their households who took them up and fled with them to the likeliest place in the hope of burial, but before it had been accomplished were pushed forward by the flames. Yet to have taken part in that agonized race for the open was worth all it cost in goods.

Before the red night paled into murky dawn thousands of people were vomited out of the angry throat of the street far down toward Market. Even the smallest child carried something, or pushed it before him on a rocking chair, or dragged it behind him in a trunk, and the thing he carried was the index of the refugee's strongest bent. All the women saved their best hats and their babies, and, if there were no babies, some of them pushed pianos up the cement pavements.

All the faces were smutched and pallid, all the figures sloped steadily forward toward the cleared places. Behind them the expelling fire bent out over the lines of flight, the writhing smoke stooped and waved, a fine rain of cinders pattered and rustled over all the folks, and charred bits of the burning fled in the heated air and dropped among the goods. There was a strange, hot, sickish smell in the street as if it had become the hollow slot of some fiery breathing snake. I came out and stood in the pale pinkish glow and saw a man I knew hurrying down toward the gutted district, the badge of a relief committee fluttering on his coat. "Bob," I said, "it looks like the day of judgment!" He cast back at me over his shoulder unveiled disgust at the inadequacy of my terms. "Aw!" he said, "it looks like hell!"

It was a well-bred community that poured itself out into Jefferson Square, where I lay with my friend's goods, and we were packed too close for most of the minor decencies, but nobody forgot his manners. "Beg pardon!" said a man hovering over me with a 200-pound trunk. "Not at all!" I answered making myself thin for him to step over. With an "Excuse me, madam!" another, fleeing from the too-heated border of the park to its packed center, deftly up-ended a roll of bedding, turned it across the woman who lay next to me—and the woman smiled.

Right here, if you had time for it, you gripped the large, essential spirit of the West, the ability to dramatize its own activity, and, while continuing in it, to stand off and be vastly entertained by it. In spite of individual heartsinkings, the San Franciscans during the week never lost the spirited sense of being audience to their own performance. Large figures of adventure moved through the murk of those days—Denman going out with his gun and holding up express wagons with expensively saved goods, which were dumped out on sidewalks that food might be carried to unfed hundreds; Father Ramm cutting away the timbers of St. Mary's tower, while the red glow crept across the charred cross out of reach of the hose; and the humble sacrifices—the woman who shared her full breast with the child of another whose fountain had failed from weariness and fright—would that I had her name to hold in remembrance! She had stopped in the middle of a long residence hill and rested on a forsaken stoop, nourishing her child quietly, when the other woman came by panting, fainting and afraid, not of her class, nor her race, but the hungry baby yearned toward the uncovered breast—and they both of them understood that speech well enough.

Everybody tells you tales like this, more, and better. All along the fire line of Van Ness Avenue, heroic episodes transpired like groups in a frieze against the writhing background of furnace-heated flame; and, for a pediment to the frieze, rows of houseless, possessionless people wrapped in a large, impersonal appreciation of the spectacle.

From Gough Street, looking down, we saw the great tide of fire roaring in the hollow toward Russian Hill burning so steadily for all it burned so fast that it had the effect of immense deliberation; roaring on toward miles of uninhabited dwellings so lately emptied of life that they appeared consciously to await their immolation; beyond the line of roofs, the hill, standing up darkly against the glow of other incalculable fires, the uplift of flames from viewless intricacies of destruction, sparks belching furiously intermittent like the spray of bursting seas. Low down in front ran besmirched Lilliputians training inadequate hose and creating tiny explosions of a block or so of expensive dwellings by which the rest of us were ultimately saved; and high against the tip of flames where it ran out in broken sparks, the figure of the priest chopping steadily at the tower with the constrained small movement of a mechanical toy.

Observe that a moment since I said houseless people, not homeless; for it comes to this with the bulk of San Franciscans, that they discovered the place and the spirit to be home rather than the walls and the furnishings. No matter how the insurance totals foot up, what landmarks, what treasures of art are evanished, San Francisco, *our* San Francisco is all there yet. Fast as the tall banners of smoke rose up and the flames reddened them, rose up with it something impalpable, like an exhalation. We saw it breaking up in the movements of the refugees, heard it in the tones of their voices, felt it as they wrestled in the teeth of destruction. The sharp sentences by which men called to each other to note the behavior of brick and stone dwellings contained a hint of a warning already accepted for the new building before the old had crumbled. When the heat of conflagration outran the flames and reaching over wide avenues caught high gables and crosses of church steeples, men watching them smoke and blister and crackle into flame, said shortly, "No more wooden towers for San Francisco!" and saved their breath to run with the hose.

What distinguishes the personal experience of the destruction of the gray city from all like disasters of record, is the keen appreciation of the deathlessness of the spirit of living. For the greater part of this disaster—the irreclaimable loss of goods and houses, the violent deaths—was due chiefly to man-contrivances, to the sinking of made ground, to huddled buildings cheapened by greed, to insensate clinging to the outer shells of life; the strong tug of nature was always toward the renewal of it. Births near their time came on hurriedly; children were delivered in the streets or the midst of burnings, and none the worse for the absence of conventional circumstance; marriages were made amazingly, as the disorder of the social world threw all men back severely upon its primal institutions.

After a great lapse of time, when earthquake stories had become matter for humorous reminiscence, burning blocks topics of daily news, and standing in the bread line a fixed habit—by the morning of the third day, to be exact—there arose a threat of peril greater than the thirst or famine, which all the world rose up swiftly to relieve.

Thousands of families had camped in parks not meant to be lived in, but to be looked at; lacking the most elementary means of sanitation. With the rising of the sun, a stench arose from these places and increased perceptibly; spreading with it like an exhalation, went the fear of pestilence. But this at least was a dread that every man could fight at his own camp, and the fight was the modern conviction of the relativity of sanitation to health. By midmorning the condition of Jefferson Square was such that I should not have trusted myself to it for three hours more, but in three hours it was made safe by no more organized effort than came of the intelligent recognition of the peril. They cleaned the camp first, and organized committees of sanitation afterward.

There have been some unconsidered references of the earthquake disaster to the judgment of God; happily not much of it, but enough to make pertinent some conclusions that shaped themselves swiftly as the city fought and ran. Not to quarrel with the intelligence that reads God behind seismic disturbance, one must still note that the actual damage done by God to the city was small beside the possibilities for damage that reside in man-contrivances; for most man-made things do inherently carry the elements of their own destruction.

How much of all that happened of distress and inestimable loss could have been averted if men would live along the line of the Original Intention, with wide, clean breathing spaces and room for green growing things to push up between?

I have an indistinct impression that the calendar time spent in the city after the temblor was about ten days. I remember the night of rain, and seeing a grown man sitting on a curbstone the morning after, sobbing in the final break-down of bodily endurance. I remember too the sigh of the wind through windows of desolate walls, and the screech and clack of ruined cornices in the red noisy night, and the cheerful banging of pianos in the camps; the burials in trenches and the little, bluish, grave-long heaps of burning among the ruins of Chinatown, and the laughter that shook us as in the midst of the ashy desert we poured in dogged stream to the ferry, at a placard that in a half-burned building where activity had begun again, swung about in the wind and displayed this legend:

DON'T TALK EARTHQUAKE
TALK BUSINESS

All these things seem to have occurred within a short space of days, but when I came out at last at Berkeley—too blossomy, too full-leafed, too radiant—by this token I knew that a great hiatus had taken place. It had been long enough to forget that the smell of sun-steeped roses could be sweet.

from *Lost Borders*

The Return of Mr. Wills

Mrs. Wills had lived seventeen years with Mr. Wills, and when he left her for three, those three were so much the best of her married life that she wished he had never come back. And the only real trouble with Mr. Wills was that he should never have moved West. Back East I suppose they breed such men because they need them, but they ought really to keep them there.

I am quite certain that when Mr. Wills was courting Mrs. Wills he parted his hair in the middle, and the breast-pocket of his best suit had a bright silk lining which Mr. Wills pulled up to simulate a silk handkerchief. Mrs. Wills had a certain draggled prettiness, and a way of tossing her head which came back to her after Mr. Wills left, which made you think she might have been the prettiest girl of her town. They were happy enough at first, when Mr. Wills was a grocery clerk, assistant Sunday-school superintendent, and they owned a cabinet organ and four little Willses. It might have been that Mr. Wills thought he could go right on being the same sort of a man in the West—he was clerk at the Bed Rock Emporium, and had brought the organ and the children; or it might have been at bottom he thought himself a very different sort of man, and meant to be it if he got a chance.

There is a sort of man bred up in close communities, like a cask, to whom the church, public opinion, the social note, are a sort of hoop to hold him in serviceable shape. Without these there are a good many ways of going to pieces. Mr. Wills' way was Lost Mines.

Being clerk at the Emporium, where miners and prospectors bought their supplies, he heard a lot of talk about mines, and was too new to it to understand that the man who has the most time to stop and talk about it has the least to do with mining. And of all he heard, the most fascinating to Mr. Wills, who was troubled with an imagination, was of the lost mines: incredibly rich ledges, touched and not found again. To go out into the unmapped hills on the mere chance of coming across something was, on the face of it, a risky business; but to look for a mine once located, sampled and proved, definitely situated in a particular mountain range or a certain cañon, had a smack of plausibility. Besides that, an ordinary prospect might or might not prove workable, but the lost mines were always amazingly rich. Of all the ways in the West for a man to go to pieces this is the most insidious. Out there beyond the towns the long Wilderness lies brooding, imperturbable; she puts out to adventurous minds glittering fragments of fortune or romance, like the lures men use to catch antelopes—clip! then she has them. If Mr. Wills had gambled or drank, his wife could have gone to the minister about it, his friends could have done something. There was a church in Maverick of twenty-seven members, and the Willses had brought letters to it, but except for the effect it had on Mrs. Wills, it would not be worth mentioning. Though he might never have found it out in the East, Mr. Wills belonged to the church, not because of what it meant to himself, but for what it meant to other people. Back East it had meant social standing, repute, moral impeccability. To other people in Maverick it meant a weakness which was excused in you so long as you did not talk about it. Mr. Wills did not, because there was so much else to talk about in connection with lost mines.

He began by grub-staking Pedro Ruiz to look for the Lost Ledge of Fisherman's Peak, and that was not so bad, for it had not been lost more than thirty years, the peak was not a hundred miles from Maverick, and, besides, I have a piece of the ore myself. Then he was bitten by the myth of the Gunsight, of which there was never anything more tangible than a dime's worth of virgin silver, picked up by a Jayhawker, hammered into a sight for a gun; and you had to take the gun on faith at that, for it and the man who owned it had quite disappeared; and afterward it was the Duke o' Wild Rose, which was never a mine at all, merely an arrow-mark on a map left by a penniless lodger found dead in a San Francisco hotel. Grub-staking is expensive, even to a clerk at the Bed Rock Emporium getting discounts on the grub, and grub-staked prospectors are about as dependable as the dreams they chase, often pure fakes, lying up at seldom-visited waterholes while the stake lasts, returning with wilder tales and clews more alluring. It was a late conviction that led Mr. Wills, when he put the last remnant of his means into the search for the White Cement mines, to resign his clerkship and go in charge of the expedition himself. There is no doubt whatever that there is a deposit of cement on Bald Mountain, with lumps of gold sticking out of it like plums in a pudding. It lies at the bottom of a small gulch near the middle fork of Owens River, and is overlaid by pumice. There is a camp kit buried somewhere near, and two skeletons. There is also an Indian in that vicinity who is thought to be able to point out the exact location—if he would. It is quite the sort of thing to appeal to the imagination of Mr. Wills, and he spent two years proving that he could not find it. After that he drifted out toward the Lee district to look for Lost Cabin mine, because a man who had immediate need of twenty dollars, had, for that amount, offered Wills some exact and unpublished information as to its location. By that time Wills' movements had ceased to interest anybody in Maverick. He could be got to believe anything about any sort of a prospect, providing it was lost.

The only visible mark left by all this was on Mrs. Wills. Everybody in a mining-town, except the minister and professional gamblers who wear frock-coats, dresses pretty much alike, and Wills very soon got to wear in his face the guileless, trustful fixity of the confirmed prospector. It seemed as if the desert had overshot him and struck at Mrs. Wills, and Richard Wills, Esther Wills, Benjy Wills, and the youngest Wills, who was called Mugsey. Desertness attacked the door-yard and the house; even the cabinet organ had a weathered look. During the time of the White Cement obsession the Wills family appeared to be in need of a grub-stake themselves. Mrs. Wills' eyes were like the eyes of trail-weary cattle; her hands grew to have that pitiful way of catching the front of her dress of the woman not so much a slattern as hopeless. It was when her husband went out after Lost Cabin she fell into the habit of sitting down to a cheap novel with the dishes unwashed, a sort of drugging of despair common among women of the camps. All this time Mr. Wills was drifting about from camp to camp of the desert borders, working when it could not be avoided, but mostly on long, fruitless trudges among the unmindful ranges. I do not know if the man was honest with himself; if he knew by this time that the clew of a lost mine was the baldest of excuses merely to be out and away from everything that savored of definiteness and responsibility. The fact was, the desert had got him. All the hoops were off the cask. The mind of Mr. Wills faded out at the edges like the desert horizon that melts in mists and mirages, and finally he went on an expedition from which he did not come back.

He had been gone nearly a year when Mrs. Wills gave up expecting him. She had grown so used to the bedraggled crawl of life that she might never have taken any notice of the disappearance of Mr. Wills had not the Emporium refused to make any more charges in his name. There had been a great many dry water-holes on the desert that year, and more than the usual complement of sun-dried corpses. In a general way this accounted for Mr. Wills, though nothing transpired of sufficient definiteness to justify Mrs. Wills in putting on a widow's dress, and, anyway, she could not have afforded it.

Mrs. Wills and the children went to work, and work was about the only thing in Maverick of which there was more than enough. It was a matter of a very few months when Mrs. Wills made the remarkable discovery that after the family bills were paid at the end of the month, there was a little over. A very little. Mrs. Wills had lived so long with the tradition that a husband is a natural provider that it took some months longer to realize that she not only did not need Mr. Wills, but got on better without him. This was about the time she was able to have the sitting-room repapered and put up lace curtains. And the next spring the children planted roses in the front yard. All up and down the wash of Salt Creek there were lean coyote mothers, and wild folk of every sort could have taught her that nature never makes the mistake of neglecting to make the child-bearer competent to provide. But Mrs. Wills had not been studying life in the lairs. She had most of her notions of it from the church and her parents, and all under the new sense of independence and power she had an ache of forlornness and neglect. As a matter of fact she filled out, grew stronger, had a spring

in her walk. She was not pining for Mr. Wills; the desert had him—
for whatever conceivable use, it was more than Mrs. Wills could put
him to—let the desert keep what it had got.

It was in the third summer that she regained a certain air that
made me think she must have been pretty when Mr. Wills married
her. And no woman in a mining-town can so much as hint at prettiness without its being found out. Mrs. Wills had a good many prejudices left over from the time when Mr. Wills had been superintendent of the Sunday-school, and would not hear of divorce. Yet, as the
slovenliness of despair fell away from her, as she held up her head and
began to have company to tea, it is certain somebody would have
broached it to her before the summer was over; but by that time Mr.
Wills came back.

It happened that Benjy Wills, who was fourteen and driving the
Bed Rock delivery wagon, had a runaway accident in which he had
behaved very handsomely and gotten a fractured skull. News of it
went by way of the local paper to Tonopah, and from there drifted
south to the Funeral Mountains and the particular prospect that
Mr. Wills was working on a grub-stake. He had come to that.
Perhaps as much because he had found there was nothing in it, as
from paternal anxiety, he came home the evening of the day the
doctor had declared the boy out of danger.

It was my turn to sit up that night, I remember, and Mrs. Meyer,
who had the turn before, was telling me about the medicines. There
was a neighbor woman who had come in by the back door with a
bowl of custard, and the doctor standing in the sitting-room with
Mrs. Wills, when Mr. Wills came in through the black block of the
doorway with his hand before his face to ward off the light—and
perhaps some shamefacedness—who knows?

I saw Mrs. Wills quiver, and her hand went up to her bosom as if some
one had struck her. I have seen horses start and check like that as they
came over the Pass and the hot blast of the desert took them fairly. It was
the stroke of desolation. I remember turning quickly at the doctor's curt
signal to shut the door between the sitting-room and Benjy.

"Don't let the boy see you to-night, Wills," said the doctor, with
no hint of a greeting; "he's not to be excited." With that he got himself off as quickly as possible, and the neighbor woman and I went

out and sat on the back steps a long time, and tried to talk about everything but Mr. Wills. When I went in, at last, he was sitting in the Morris chair, which had come with soap-wrappers, explaining to Mrs. Meyer about the rich prospect he had left to come to his darling boy. But he did not get so much as a glimpse of his darling boy while I was in charge.

Mr. Wills settled on his family like a blight. For a man who has prospected lost mines to that extent is positively not good for anything else. It was not only as if the desert had sucked the life out of him and cast him back, but as if it would have Mrs. Wills in his room. As the weeks went on you could see a sort of dinginess creeping up from her dress to her hair and her face, and it spread to the house and the doorway. Mr. Wills had enjoyed the improved condition of his home, though he missed the point of it; his wife's cooking tasted good to him after miner's fare, and he was proud of his boys. He didn't want any more of the desert. Not he. "There's no place like home," said Mr. Wills, or something to that effect.

But he had brought the desert with him on his back. If it had been at any other time than when her mind was torn with anxiety for Benjy, Mrs. Wills might have made a fight against it. But the only practical way to separate the family from the blight was to divorce Mr. Wills, and the church to which Mrs. Wills belonged admitted divorce only in the event of there being another woman.

Mrs. Wills rose to the pitch of threatening, I believe, about the time Mr. Wills insisted on his right to control the earnings of his sons. But the minister called; the church put out its hand upon her poor, staggered soul that sunk aback. The minister himself was newly from the East, and did not understand that the desert is to be dealt with as a woman and a wanton; he was thinking of it as a place on the map. Therefore, he was not of the slightest use to Mrs. Wills, which did not prevent him from commanding her behavior. And the power of the wilderness lay like a wasting sickness on the home.

About that time Mrs. Wills took to novel-reading again; the eldest son drifted off up Tonopah way; and Benjy began to keep back a part of the wages he brought home. And Mr. Wills is beginning to collect misinformation about the exact locality where Peg-leg Smith is supposed to have found the sunburnt nuggets. He does not mention the matter often, being, as he says, done with mines; but whenever the Peg-leg comes up in talk I can see Mrs. Wills chirk up a little, her gaze wandering to the inscrutable grim spaces, not with the hate you might suppose, but with something like hope in her eye, as if she had guessed what I am certain of—that in time its insatiable spirit will reach out and take Mr. Wills again.

And this time, if I know Mrs. Wills, he will not come back.

The Readjustment

Emma Jeffries had been dead and buried three days. The sister who had come to the funeral had taken Emma's child away with her, and the house was swept and aired; then, when it seemed there was least occasion for it, Emma came back. The neighbor woman who had nursed her was the first to know it. It was about seven of the evening in a mellow gloom: the neighbor woman was sitting on her own stoop with her arms wrapped in her apron, and all at once she found herself going along the street under an urgent sense that Emma needed her. She was half-way down the block before she recollected that this was impossible, for Mrs. Jeffries was dead and buried; but as soon as she came opposite the house she was aware of what had happened. It was all open to the summer air; except that it was a little neater, not otherwise than the rest of the street. It was quite dark; but the presence of Emma Jeffries streamed from it and betrayed it more than a candle. It streamed out steadily across the garden, and even as it reached her, mixed with the smell of the damp mignonette, the neighbor woman owned to herself that she had always known Emma would come back.

"A sight stranger if she wouldn't," thought the woman who had nursed her. "She wasn't ever one to throw off things easily."

Emma Jeffries had taken death as she had taken everything in life, hard. She had met it with the same bright, surface competency that she had presented to the squalor of the encompassing desertness, to the insuperable commonness of Sim Jeffries, to the affliction of her crippled child; and the intensity of her wordless struggle against it had caught the attention of the townspeople and held it in a shocked curious awe. She was so long a-dying, lying there in that little low house, hearing the abhorred footsteps going about her rooms and the vulgar procedure of the community encroach upon her like the advances of the sand wastes on an unwatered field. For Emma had always wanted things different, wanted them with a fury of intentness that implied offensiveness in things as they were. And the townspeople had taken offence, the more so because she was not to be surprised in any inaptitude for their own kind of success. Do what you could, you could never catch Emma Jeffries in a wrapper after three o'clock in the afternoon. And she would never talk about the child—in a country where so little ever happened that even trouble was a godsend if it gave you something to talk about. It was reported that she did not even talk to Sim. But there the common resentment got back at her. If she had thought to effect anything with Sim Jeffries against the benumbing spirit of the place, the evasive hopefulness, the large sense of leisure that ungirt the loins, if she still hoped somehow to get away with him to some place for which by her dress, by her manner, she seemed forever and unassailably fit, it was foregone that nothing would come of it. They knew Sim Jeffries better than that. Yet so vivid had been the force of her wordless dissatisfaction that when the fever took her and she went down like a pasteboard figure in the damp, the wonder was that nothing toppled with her. And, as if she too had felt herself indispensable, Emma Jeffries had come back.

The neighbor woman crossed the street, and as she passed the far corner of the garden, Jeffries spoke to her. He had been standing, she did not know how long a time, behind the syringa-bush, and moved even with her along the fence until they came to the gate. She could see in the dusk that before speaking he wet his lips with his tongue.

"She's in there," he said, at last.

"Emma?"

He nodded. "I been sleeping at the store since—but I thought I'd be more comfortable—as soon as I opened the door there she was."

"Did you see her?"

"No."

"How do you know, then?"

"Don't you know?"

The neighbor felt there was nothing to say to that.

"Come in," he whispered, huskily. They slipped by the rose-tree and the wistaria, and sat down on the porch at the side. A door swung inward behind them. They felt the Presence in the dusk beating like a pulse.

"What do you think she wants?" said Jeffries. "Do you reckon it's the boy?"

"Like enough."

"He's better off with his aunt. There was no one here to take care of him like his mother wanted." He raised his voice unconsciously with a note of justification, addressing the room behind.

"I am sending fifty dollars a month," he said; "he can go with the best of them."

He went on at length to explain all the advantage that was to come to the boy from living at Pasadena, and the neighbor woman bore him out in it.

"He was glad to go," urged Jeffries to the room. "He said it was what his mother would have wanted."

They were silent then a long time, while the Presence seemed to swell upon them and encroached upon the garden.

Finally, "I gave Ziegler the order for the monument yesterday," Jeffries threw out, appeasingly. "It's to cost three hundred and fifty."

The Presence stirred. The neighbor thought she could fairly see the controlled tolerance with which Emma Jeffries endured the evidence of Sim's ineptitudes.

They sat on helplessly without talking after that until the woman's husband came to the fence and called her.

"Don't go," begged Sim.

"Hush," she said. "Do you want all the town to know? You had naught but good from Emma living, and no call to expect harm from her now. It's natural she should come back—if—if she was lonesome like—in—the place where she's gone to."

"Emma wouldn't come back to this place," Jeffries protested, "without she wanted something."

"Well, then, you've got to find out," said the neighbor woman.

All the next day she saw, whenever she passed the house, that Emma was still there. It was shut and barred, but the Presence lurked behind the folded blinds and fumbled at the doors. When it was night and the moths began in the columbine under the windows, it went out and walked in the garden.

Jeffries was waiting at the gate when the neighbor woman came.

He sweated with helplessness in the warm dusk, and the Presence brooded upon them like an apprehension that grows by being entertained.

"She wants something," he appealed, "but I can't make out what. Emma knows she is welcome to everything I've got. Everybody knows I've been a good provider."

The neighbor woman remembered suddenly the only time she had ever drawn close to Emma Jeffries touching the boy. They had sat up with it together all one night in some childish ailment, and she had ventured a question. "What does his father think?" And Emma had turned her a white, hard face of surpassing dreariness.

"I don't know," she admitted, "he never says."

"There's more than providing," suggested the neighbor woman.

"Yes. There's feeling...but she had enough to do to put up with me. I had no call to be troubling her with such." He left off to mop his forehead, and began again.

"Feelings!" he said, "there's times a man gets so wore out with feelings he doesn't have them any more."

He talked, and presently it grew clear to the woman that he was voiding all the stuff of his life, as if he had sickened on it and was now done. It was a little soul knowing itself and not good to see. What was singular was that the Presence left off walking in the garden, came and caught like a gossamer on the ivy-tree, swayed by the breath of his broken sentences. He talked, and the neighbor woman saw him for once as he saw himself and Emma, snared and floundering in an inexplicable unhappiness. He had been disappointed, too. She had never relished the man he was, and it made him ashamed. That was why he had never gone away, lest he should make her ashamed among her own kind. He was her husband, he could not help that though he was sorry for it. But he could keep the offence where least was made of it. And there was a child—she had wanted a child; but even then he had blundered—begotten a cripple upon her. He blamed himself utterly, searched out the roots of his youth for the answer to that, until the neighbor woman flinched to hear him. But the Presence stayed.

He had never talked to his wife about the child. How should he? There was the fact—the advertisement of his incompetence. And she had never talked to him. That was the one blessed and unassailable memory; that she had spread silence like a balm over his hurt. In return for it he had never gone away. He had resisted her that he might save her from showing among her own kind how poor a man he was. With every word of this ran the fact of his love for her—as he had loved her, with all the stripes of clean and uncleanness. He bared himself as a child without knowing; and the Presence stayed. The talk trailed off at last to the commonplaces of consolation between the retchings of his spirit. The Presence lessened and streamed toward them on the wind of the garden. When it touched them like the warm air of noon that lies sometimes in hollow places after nightfall, the neighbor woman rose and went away.

The next night she did not wait for him. When a rod outside the town—it was a very little one—the burrowing owls *whoo-whooed*, she hung up her apron and went to talk with Emma Jeffries. The Presence was there, drawn in, lying close. She found the key between the wistaria and the first pillar of the porch, but as soon as she opened the door she felt the chill that might be expected by one intruding on Emma Jeffries in her own house.

"'The Lord is my shepherd,'" said the neighbor woman; it was the first religious phrase that occurred to her; then she said the whole of the psalm and after that a hymn. She had come in through the door and stood with her back to it and her hand upon the knob. Everything was just as Mrs. Jeffries had left it, with the waiting air of a room kept for company.

"Em," she said, boldly, when the chill had abated a little before the sacred words. "Em Jeffries, I've got something to say to you. And you've got to hear," she added with firmness, as the white curtains stirred duskily at the window. "You wouldn't be talked to about your troubles when…you were here before; and we humored you. But now there is Sim to be thought of. I guess you heard what you came for last night, and got good of it. Maybe it would have been better if Sim had said things all along instead of hoarding them in his heart, but any way he has said them now. And what I want to say is, if you was staying on with the hope of hearing it again, you'd be making a mistake. You was an uncommon woman, Emma Jeffries, and there didn't none of us understand you very well, nor do you justice maybe; but Sim is only a common man, and I understand him because I'm that way myself. And if you think he'll be opening his heart to you every night, or be any different from what he's always been on account of what's happened, that's a mistake too…and in a little while, if you stay, it will be as bad as it always was. Men are like that…You'd better go now while there's understanding between you." She stood staring into the darkling room that seemed suddenly full of turbulence and denial. It seemed to beat upon her and take her breath, but she held on.

"You've got to go…Em…and I'm going to stay until you do." She said this with finality, and then began again.

"'The Lord is nigh unto them that are of a broken heart,'" and repeated the passage to the end. Then as the Presence sank before it. "You better go, Emma," persuasively, and again after an interval:

"'He shall deliver thee in six troubles, yea, in seven shall no evil touch thee.'"

…The Presence gathered itself and was still. She could make out that it stood over against the opposite corner by the gilt easel with the crayon portrait of the child.

…"'For thou shalt forget thy misery. Thou shalt remember it as waters that are past,'" concluded the neighbor woman, as she heard Jeffries on the gravel outside. What the Presence had wrought upon him in the night was visible in his altered mien. He looked more than anything else to be in need of sleep. He had eaten his sorrow, and that was the end of it—as it is with men.

"I came to see if there was anything I could do for you," said the woman, neighborly, with her hand upon the door.

"I don't know as there is," said he; "I'm much obliged, but I don't know as there is."

"You see," whispered the woman over her shoulder, "not even to me." She felt the tug of her heart as the Presence swept past her.

The neighbor went out after that and walked in the ragged street, past the school-house, across the creek below the town, out by the fields, over the headgate, and back by the town again. It was full nine of the clock when she passed the Jeffries house. It looked, except for being a little neater, not other than the rest of the street. The door was open and the lamp was lit; she saw Jeffries, black against it. He sat reading in a book, like a man at ease in his own house.

The Walking Woman

The first time of my hearing of her was at Temblor. We had come all one day between blunt, whitish bluffs rising from mirage water, with a thick, pale wake of dust billowing from the wheels, all the dead wall of the foothills sliding and shimmering with heat, to learn that the Walking Woman had passed us somewhere in the dizzying dimness, going down to the Tulares on her own feet. We heard of her again in the Carrisal, and again at Adobe Station, where she had passed a week before the shearing, and at last I had a glimpse of her at the Eighteen-Mile House as I went hurriedly northward on the Mojave stage; and afterward sheepherders at whose camps she slept, and cowboys at rodeos, told me as much of her way of life as they could understand. Like enough they told her as much of mine. That was very little. She was the Walking Woman, and no one knew her name, but because she was a sort of whom men speak respectfully, they called her to her face Mrs. Walker, and she answered to it if she was so inclined. She came and went about our western world on no discoverable errand, and whether she had some place of refuge where she lay by in the interim, or whether between her seldom, unaccountable appearances in our quarter she went on steadily walking, we never learned. She came and went, oftenest in a kind of muse of travel which the untrammelled space begets, or at rare intervals flooding wondrously with talk, never of herself, but of things she had known and seen. She must have seen some rare happenings, too—by report. She was at Maverick the time of the Big Snow, and at Tres Piños when they brought home the body of Morena; and if anybody could have told whether De Borba killed Mariana for spite or defence, it would have been she, only she could not be found when most wanted. She was at Tunawai

at the time of the cloud-burst, and if she had cared for it could have
known most desirable things of the ways of trail-making, burrow-
habiting small things.

All of which should have made her worth meeting, though it
was not, in fact, for such things I was wishful to meet her; and as it
turned out, it was not of these things we talked when at last we
came together. For one thing, she was a woman, not old, who had
gone about alone in a country where the number of women is as
one in fifteen. She had eaten and slept at the herder's camps, and
laid by for days at one-man stations whose masters had no other
touch of human kind than the passing of chance prospectors, or the
halting of the tri-weekly stage. She had been set on her way by
teamsters who lifted her out of white, hot desertness and put her
down at the crossing of unnamed ways, days distant from anywhere. And through all this she passed unarmed and unoffended. I
had the best testimony to this, the witness of the men themselves. I
think they talked of it because they were so much surprised at it. It
was not, on the whole, what they expected of themselves.

Well I understand that nature which wastes its borders with too
eager burning, beyond which rim of desolation it flares forever
quick and white, and have had some inkling of the isolating calm
of a desire too high to stoop to satisfaction. But you could not think
of these things pertaining to the Walking Woman; and if there were
ever any truth in the exemption from offence residing in a frame of
behavior called ladylike, it should have been inoperative here.
What this really means is that you get no affront so long as your
behavior in the estimate of the particular audience invites none. In
the estimate of the immediate audience—conduct which affords
protection in Mayfair gets you no consideration in Maverick. And
by no canon could it be considered ladylike to go about on your
own feet, with a blanket and a black bag and almost no money in
your purse, in and about the haunts of rude and solitary men.

There were other things that pointed the wish for a personal
encounter with the Walking Woman. One of them was the contra-
diction of reports of her—as to whether she was comely, for example. Report said yes, and again, plain to the point of deformity. She
had a twist to her face, some said; a hitch to one shoulder; they

averred she limped as she walked. But by the distance she covered she should have been straight and young. As to sanity, equal incertitude. On the mere evidence of her way of life she was cracked; not quite broken, but unserviceable. Yet in her talk there was both wisdom and information, and the word she brought about trails and water-holes was as reliable as an Indian's.

By her own account she had begun by walking off an illness. There had been an invalid to be taken care of for years, leaving her at last broken in body, and with no recourse but her own feet to carry her out of that predicament. It seemed there had been, besides the death of her invalid, some other worrying affairs, upon which, and the nature of her illness, she was never quite clear, so that it might very well have been an unsoundness of mind which drove her to the open, sobered and healed at last by the large soundness of nature. It must have been about that time that she lost her name. I am convinced that she never told it because she did not know it herself. She was the Walking Woman, and the country people called her Mrs. Walker. At the time I knew her, though she wore short hair and a man's boots, and had a fine down over all her face from exposure to the weather, she was perfectly sweet and sane.

I had met her occasionally at ranch-houses and road-stations, and had got as much acquaintance as the place allowed; but for the things I wished to know there wanted a time of leisure and isolation. And when the occasion came we talked altogether of other things.

It was at Warm Spring in the Little Antelope I came upon her in the heart of a clear forenoon. The spring lies off a mile from the main trail, and has the only trees about it known in that country. First you come upon a pool of waste full of weeds of a poisonous dark green, every reed ringed about the water-level with a muddy white incrustation. Then the three oaks appear staggering on the slope, and the spring sobs and blubbers below them in ashy-colored mud. All the hills of that country have the down plunge toward the desert and back abruptly toward the Sierra. The grass is thick and brittle and bleached straw-color toward the end of the season. As I rode up the swale of the spring I saw the Walking Woman sitting where the grass was deepest, with her black bag and blanket, which she carried on a stick, beside her. It was one of those days when the genius of talk flows as smoothly as the rivers of mirage through the blue hot desert morning.

You are not to suppose that in my report of a Borderer I give you the words only, but the full meaning of the speech. Very often the words are merely the punctuation of thought; rather, the crests of the long waves of intercommunicative silences. Yet the speech of the Walking Woman was fuller than most.

The best of our talk that day began in some dropped word of hers from which I inferred that she had had a child. I was surprised at that, and then wondered why I should have been surprised, for it is the most natural of all experiences to have children. I said something of that purport, and also that it was one of the perquisites of living I should be least willing to do without. And that led to the Walking Woman saying that there were three things which if you had known you could cut out all the rest, and they were good any way you got them, but best if, as in her case, they were related to and grew each one out of the others. It was while she talked that I decided that she really did have a twist to her face, a sort of natural warp or skew into which it fell when it was worn merely as a countenance, but which disappeared the moment it became the vehicle of thought or feeling.

The first of the experiences the Walking Woman had found most worth while had come to her in a sand-storm on the south slope of Tehachapi in a dateless spring. I judged it should have been about the time she began to find herself, after the period of worry and loss in which her wandering began. She had come, in a day pricked full of intimations of a storm, to the camp of Filon Geraud, whose companion shepherd had gone a three days' *pasear* to Mojave for supplies. Geraud was of great hardihood, red-blooded, of a full laughing eye, and an indubitable spark for women. It was the season of the year when there is a soft bloom on the days, but the nights are cowering cold and the lambs tender, not yet flockwise. At such times a sand-storm works incalculable disaster. The lift of the wind is so great that the whole surface of the ground appears to travel upon it slantwise, thinning out miles high in air. In the intolerable smother the lambs are lost from the ewes; neither dogs nor man make headway against it.

The morning flared through a horizon of yellow smudge, and by mid-forenoon the flock broke.

"There were but the two of us to deal with the trouble," said the Walking Woman. "Until that time I had not known how strong I was, nor how good it is to run when running is worth while. The flock travelled down the wind, the sand bit our faces; we called, and after a time heard the words broken and beaten small by the wind. But after a little we had not to call. All the time of our running in the yellow dusk of day and the black dark of night, I knew where Filon was. A flock-length away, I knew him. Feel? What should I feel? I knew. I ran with the flock and turned it this way and that as Filon would have.

"Such was the force of the wind that when we came together we held by one another and talked a little between pantings. We snatched and ate what we could as we ran. All that day and night until the next afternoon the camp kit was not out of the cayaques. But we held the flock. We herded them under a butte when the wind fell off a little, and the lambs sucked; when the storm rose they broke, but we kept upon their track and brought them together again. At night the wind quieted, and we slept by turns; at least Filon slept. I lay on the ground when my turn was and beat with the storm. I was no more tired than the earth was. The sand filled in the creases of the blanket, and where I turned, dripped back upon the ground. But we saved the sheep. Some ewes there were that would not give down their milk because of the worry of the storm, and the lambs died. But we kept the flock together. And I was not tired."

The Walking Woman stretched out her arms and clasped herself, rocking in them as if she would have hugged the recollection to her breast.

"For you see," said she, "I worked with a man, without excusing, without any burden on me of looking or seeming. Not fiddling or fumbling as women work, and hoping it will all turn out for the best. It was not for Filon to ask, Can you, or Will you. He said, Do, and I did. And my work was good. We held the flock. And that," said the Walking Woman, the twist coming in her face again, "is one of the things that make you able to do without the others."

"Yes," I said; and then, "What others?"

"Oh," she said, as if it pricked her, "the looking and the seeming."

And I had not thought until that time that one who had the courage to be the Walking Woman would have cared! We sat and looked at the pattern of the thick crushed grass on the slope, wavering in the fierce noon like the waterings in the coat of a tranquil beast; the ache of a world-old bitterness sobbed and whispered in the spring. At last—

"It is by the looking and the seeming," said I, "that the opportunity finds you out."

"Filon found out," said the Walking Woman. She smiled; and went on from that to tell me how, when the wind went down about four o'clock and left the afternoon clear and tender, the flock began to feed, and they had out the kit from the cayaques, and cooked a meal. When it was over, and Filon had his pipe between his teeth, he came over from his side of the fire, of his own notion, and stretched himself on the ground beside her. Of his own notion. There was that in the way she said it that made it seem as if nothing of the sort had happened before to the Walking Woman, and for a moment I thought she was about to tell me one of the things I wished to know; but she went on to say what Filon had said to her of her work with the flock. Obvious, kindly things, such as any man in sheer decency would have said, so that there must have something more gone with the words to make them so treasured of the Walking Woman.

"We were very comfortable," said she, "and not so tired as we expected to be. Filon leaned up on his elbow. I had not noticed until then how broad he was in the shoulders, and how strong in the arms. And we had saved the flock together. We felt that. There was something that said together, in the slope of his shoulders toward me. It was around his mouth and on the cheek high up under the shine of his eyes. And under the shine the look—the look that said, 'We are of one sort and one mind'—his eyes that were the color of the flat water in the tulares—do you know the look?"

"I know it."

"The wind was stopped and all the earth smelled of dust, and Filon understood very well that what I had done with him I could not have done so well with another. And the look—the look in the eyes—"

"Ah-ah—!"

I have always said, I will say again, I do not know why at this point the Walking Woman touched me. If it were merely a response to my unconscious throb of sympathy, or the unpremeditated way of her heart to declare that this, after all, was the best of all indispensable experiences; or if in some flash of forward vision, encompassing the unimpassioned years, the stir, the movement of tenderness were for *me*—but no; as often as I have thought of it, I have thought of a different reason, but no conclusive one, why the Walking Woman should have put out her hand and laid it on my arm.

"To work together, to love together," said the Walking Woman, withdrawing her hand again; "there you have two of the things; the other you know."

"The mouth at the breast," said I.

"The lips and the hands," said the Walking Woman. "The little, pushing hands and the small cry." There ensued a pause of fullest understanding, while the land before us swam in the noon, and a dove in the oaks behind the spring began to call. A little red fox came out of the hills and lapped delicately at the pool.

"I stayed with Filon until the fall," said she. "All that summer in the Sierras, until it was time to turn south on the trail. It was a good time, and longer than he could be expected to have loved one like me. And besides, I was no longer able to keep the trail. My baby was born in October."

Whatever more there was to say to this, the Walking Woman's hand said it, straying with remembering gesture to her breast. There are so many ways of loving and working, but only one way of the first-born. She added after an interval, that she did not know if she would have given up her walking to keep at home and tend him, or whether the thought of her son's small feet running beside her in the trails would have driven her to the open again. The baby had not stayed long enough for that. "And whenever the wind blows in the night," said the Walking Woman, "I wake and wonder if he is well covered."

She took up her black bag and her blanket; there was the ranch-house of Dos Palos to be made before night, and she went as outliers do, without a hope expressed of another meeting and no word of good-bye. She was the Walking Woman. That was it. She had walked off all sense of society-made values, and, knowing the best when the best came to her, was able to take it. Work—as I believed; love—as the Walking Woman had proved it; a child—as you sub-scribe to it. But look you: it was the naked thing the Walking Woman grasped, not dressed and tricked out, for instance, by prej-udices in favor of certain occupations; and love, man love, taken as it came, not picked over and rejected if it carried no obligation of permanency; and a child; *any* way you get it, a child is good to have, say nature and the Walking Woman; to have it and not to wait upon a proper concurrence of so many decorations that the event may not come at all.

At least one of us is wrong. To work and to love and to bear chil-dren. *That* sounds easy enough. But the way we live establishes so many things of much more importance.

Far down the dim, hot valley I could see the Walking Woman with her blanket and black bag over her shoulder. She had a queer, sidelong gait, as if in fact she had a twist all through her.

Recollecting suddenly that people called her lame, I ran down to the open place below the spring where she had passed. There in the bare, hot sand the track of her two feet bore evenly and white.

from *The Ford*

Chapter IV

Two singular and contradictory impressions mixed with Kenneth's earlier years to make up for him the sum of associative ideas called Home. One was the feeling he had about the little room where he slept. It was as safe to him as its hole to a fox. The deep adobe walls, the low roof, the pepper tree scratching comfortably about its eaves, more than all else the maternal flank of the Torr' glimpsed from its little window as from a half-opened lid, had for him the absolute quality of refuge. He came into peace there, distilled delicately as from a vase that has once held ambergris, and dropped as lightly into sleep as souls into the faith that for so long had had its daily crisis between the niches in the wall.

The other reached him from without, through the thin partition of the door that formerly had opened from it to his parents' room. It was boarded across now, and with a chintz curtain its deep recess served as a closet for his clothes, but never for the purpose for which it was probably intended, to cut him off from their private dissatisfactions. It was close to the head of his bed, and often at night, sometimes long into it, he could hear, like the wearing of machinery left to run down unattended, the guttering end of his mother's empty, unappreciative days. It had become so early part of a great natural sequence that the free, rich life of Palomitas *was* empty for his mother, that he had never attempted to account for it. He supposed it must be so with ladies. He had found himself even with a kind of tender commiseration for her in a situation so little in accord with her disposition. It drove him from his father at times to perceive in him, as he was sure she did, the source of her discomfiture, and drove him back, with a sense of their mutual incrimination, in liking heartily what a lady so beautiful and charming as his mother so completely disliked.

For they were all of them, except Mrs. Brent, wholly and absorbingly interested in what went on at Palomitas. Life for them was lived out of doors; it was only lately that the children had begun to be embarrassed by her demand that it should be in a degree lived about the supper-table or under the lamp. Days for her were to be got through somehow; they were the excuse for, or the annoying interruption to, the real performance on which, for their mother, the curtain seemed never quite to go up. There was something expected of them which they were helpless to afford her, something vaguely indicated to them by the obligation of dressing for the evening meal, of playing the piano as she was teaching Anne rather futilely to do, and particularly of talking.

"She wants us," Anne had figured it out, "to be company."

There was very little of that at Palomitas to judge by, but certainly company, under the stimulus of their mother, always talked. In their small way the children had undertaken to rise to an expectation which their father's manner ever permitted them to think of as unwarranted, but the trouble was that they *had* talked. At the Ford, by the lambing-corral, they had met the day's occasion with its appropriate comment or debate. But where, indeed,—Anne put the matter succinctly for them both,—"when you aren't doing anything, is the talk to come *from?*"

Their mother, at any rate, found an unfailing stream of it which, after the house was shut and the children in bed, ran on in a kind of fretful gurgle behind the walled-up door of Kenneth's room. It seemed to have taken on a new and sharpening impetus after the return of the Burkes from Summerfield. They had come driving down the Draw after a week's absence with a distinct and distinctly maintained air of having been in the great world, to set up in this quiet cove of Tierra Longa an eddy of its tremendous stir. Things were doing out there, things which, even with his salaried position and perquisites, Mr. Burke thought it a pity a man should miss, things which he permitted them to guess rather than directly said, he had been sent for in order that he shouldn't miss. Treasures were being pumped up out of the earth, trips to Europe, houses in the city; better still, enlarged opportunities for involving yourself in the stir, for making, to a degree, a stir on your own account.

"Makes a man feel like he was *in* things," he confessed, "money passing like that; even if it doesn't stick to you none, you feel it circulating." He seemed freshened and livened by the touch; he even handed it about for the moment to his hearers.

"You mean to tell us, then, that none of it *did* stick to you?" Mrs. Brent was watching him, Kenneth thought, almost as if she expected to detect it somewhere about his person.

Cornelius Burke was a tall, bony man with the blue, black-fringed Irish eyes which he had managed to pass on to Virginia without implicating her in the nose and chin between which a Fenian conspiracy was deferred by a bristling, square-cut, black mustache. His admiration for Mrs. Brent as a fine figure of a woman was just modified by resentment at her restless maternal anxiety. It was an implication of Brent's inability to bring his affairs to a successful issue, which as Brent's friend he was unwilling to admit. He dropped back, at her question, from neighborliness to his character of cautious agent.

"You have to be *in* the game for that…those yellow birds don't perch, I reckon, except where there's bird lime about. Not but what I'd be above taking a whirl if it came my way," he relaxed, remembering Virginia.

"You think, then, that it's a sound development, that it will hold out as it's begun?" Brent questioned. "These things have a way of slumping."

Burke grinned. "It won't slump yet a while, I can tell you. The Old Man's in deep. Deep."

Although they might have questioned its legitimacy, no one in his senses would have doubted the financial fatness of any venture so long as the Old Man remained in it. And the extent to which he was "in" was proclaimed very loudly within the week by the "Summerfield Clarion," and in Tierra Longa more personally by the fact that he had not discouraged, as his habit was, the favored ones in his employ from taking stock in the enterprises which circulated in his name, but even condescended so far as to indicate the companies in which he deemed it advisable stock should be taken. He had spread at last, as Tierra Longa had lingeringly hoped, as it believed he might so easily and humanly do, the mantle of his financial competency over their insufficiencies. It produced in certain of the community a kind of pocket loyalty, a disposition to find in the methods by which Agua Caliente had been compacted, out of two or three loose-titled Spanish grants, into one of the best cattle ranches in the country, nothing more reprehensible than the acumen upon which the success of their investments now hung. Wasn't the very relentlessness with which he had hemmed in and starved, and at the psychological moment finally bought out settlers in the adjacent grazing-lands, the best of evidence that he would be able to maintain his interests in the oil field? It was all a question of whether you were against the Old Man in this game, or with him. If until now you had found yourself in the first case, you could at least measure by it what might be coming to you in the second, if, as seemed wondrously the fact, he had decided to let you "in" on his oil ventures. All down the valley farms, and in the hill coves from which he had not yet successfully dislodged the preëmptors, there ran the welding warmth which money makes, passing from hand to hand. At Palomitas it was felt, however, that they were unfairly and inexplicably out of it.

"We always *will* be, as long as you insist on living in a place like this," Mrs. Brent would protest to her husband in the biting hours when she worked off against him the energies undischarged by tasks which she made it a peculiar merit not to do. "Though I do live in the country, I don't have to *be* country," she had professed to Mrs. Burke. "A woman has to keep up a standard; she has only herself to thank if she lets herself down." And how beautifully, by the aid of paper patterns and the mail-order catalogues, she had kept up, she was as willing to have known as to be commiserated on the extent to which her family weren't able to keep up with her.

"I don't see," she would offer to her husband's heavy-eyed attention, "what we are living here *for*, if it isn't to find ourselves in a position to take advantage of such opportunities when they come along. And how *can* we when all we get by living here is just *living?*"

"It's all, my dear, we'd get by living anywhere, isn't it?" Brent had ventured.

"Oh! if you call this living! It's merely being alive. And the

children; I'd like to know what *they* are to get out of it. You never
seem to think of *them*. Not even a decent school."

She had him there, as Mr. Brent's silence seemed to imply. He
wanted the best for his children.

"Even if you haven't any compunction about throwing *my* life
away," she followed up, "you might think of Anne! I suppose I can't
even take her to the coast this year."

"If you did," he reminded her, "she wouldn't in that case have got
any schooling either."

"Oh, they'll get nothing whatever, either of them. I suppose I'll
have to make up my mind to that!"

He had nothing, however, to offer her but the hope, dulled by
much handling, of "getting things straightened out," of "seeing his
way" to something which would be a little more commensurate
with what she felt herself so richly entitled to. He wasn't, if you
came down to cases, he reminded her again, getting so much out of
it himself. That touched upon the half-sensitized root of wifeliness.

"It's not "—she fell back upon the note of renunciation—"that I
mind doing without things, if it only came to anything. I shouldn't
mind not going anywhere, if I had the *price* of going to spend on
something I liked better. But I've *been* doing without...and now
where are we?" Her voice would break with it, the vexation, the sin-
cerity of her effort and the futility of it, to lay hold on anything in
her situation that approximated to what, for her, were the values of
life. "It isn't as if I didn't do my part, Steven...the only part this
kind of life gives me a chance for. I've kept friendly with the
Burkes—a regular Biddy she'd be if it wasn't for Cornelius—and
what I've done for Frank...His father would be sure to put you on
to something if only—Oh, it is too *stupid* for anything..."

Sentences like these ran on and mingled in the boy's mind with
the tinkle of water dropping from the flume and the riffle of the
wind across the chaparral by which the Torr' seemed to breathe. In
that impressionable hour between the day and dark, the two
streams sunk and watered the roots of being. Day by day, as the
rains held off and the year declared itself one of unrelievable
drought, a note of desperation crept into the question and recrimi-
nation that went on behind the walled-up door.

Early in April the curse of *el año malo* began to settle down upon
Tierra Longa, to be felt even by the children. Both at Agua Caliente
and Palomitas they were selling off as many wethers and yearlings
as possible on account of the scarcity of feed. For three days buyers
from San Francisco had been at the ranch across the river, and now
the drive was beginning; far down the road to Arroyo Verde the
children could count the columns of dust where they went in
bands of three hundred. In the flat below, the shepherds were still
busy parting out the ewes; they spread, white from the recent shearing, scattering, like grains of corn in the popper, up the coast-wise
slope. The Palomitas's yearlings had been turned out of the fenced
pastures below the house, and far toward Saltillo the lamb-band fed
under Juan Romero, outside the fence.

All down the east side of the valley below the Brent ranch, the
range was government land, with here and there a quarter-section
bought by the owner of Agua Caliente from the hardy homestead-
er who had wasted five years upon it. Just which of the unfenced
squares were owned thus was a matter of conjecture, but enough of
them to keep out the wandering herders who passed in their yearly
round along the Saltillo hills. It was so easy for the owner of land,
that had been inadvertently grazed upon, to institute a claim for
damages that pared the profits of a whole year's herding. On dry
years the knee-high sage and the curled dry "fillaree" between was
not thought worth the risk. That was why, when it had been determined to turn the Palomitas flocks on the unclaimed public pasture, they had been put in charge of Juan Romero, who knew—not
even the buzzards knew better—just which of the invisibly divided squares had passed into private ownership.

It was reported, indeed, that Romero, as the last of the generation
who had received the original grant of Agua Caliente directly from
the Spanish Crown, knew more of its titles and boundaries than it
would be convenient for the Old Man to have made public. What
he might or mightn't have got out of the Old Man on account of it
had been for long one of the settled speculations of Arroyo Verde.

The drought crept on them slowly. The spring flood came too
early, with the rapidly melting snows, and was gone too soon. The
wild grass failed to seed: the buzzards thickened in the lit space

between the ranges. The one good rain which was to have saved them dissolved in quick, impotent showers; by the end of June the streams were all shrunk well within their summer limits. Over all Tierra Longa a weight like a great hand was laid, moving up slowly toward the source of life and breath.

It turned out that, though there was no school at Palomitas, it made very little difference to Kenneth; he was to be kept at the herding. He remembered his father's curt "I can't spare him" as the point at which he began to react instinctively to the pressure from without, the impalpable threatening of the Powers. Whatever it was, he felt himself leagued with his father not to let it happen. Two of the men had been paid off early in the season; there were days when it did not seem possible one pair of legs could do all the running necessary to keep the hungry sheep at their short pastures. Evenings Kenneth would drop asleep with fatigue over his plate, starting awake with a feeling of his mother's immense and inexplicable graciousness in not taking it out of him for such lapses. Times he would be conscious of her hands about him as she laid him on his bed, and moved his lips gratefully against her sleeve, her bosom...

Anne, it had been decided, should ride over every day to have lessons with Virginia and Frank under the young tutor. Afternoons Frank would ride back with her to open the gates. The tutor modestly confided to Mrs. Brent that this was partly his own idea; he considered the society of girls excellent for Frank; it was softening. Much of his own softness, which was conspicuous, he owed to such influences. The tutor had not, however, seen his young charges racing up the lane with flying hair and lathered horses. Mrs. Brent had, and made it the basis of a struggle which went on the summer long between herself and Anne, in which Anne was continually losing ground. Not that Mrs. Brent debated or put commands on her. What she did was to put her into muslins and embroideries; she constrained her with nothing more palpable than paper patterns. Anne could reject the promptings of propriety with young scorn, but she was not proof against the feminine obligation of not "making wash." She was reduced by it before the end of the summer to a frame of behavior through which Kenneth could perceive the shaping outlines of a young lady. It was about this time that he noticed that his mother was not fretting about the trip to the coast with which she customarily broke the long summer at the ranch.

"I suppose I might manage it for you and Anne," his father had told her, "but I simply can't spare the boy."

"Oh," she resented, "I'm not *quite* unnatural! I don't want to spoil *all* my children's chances!"

Kenneth took it from this that Anne was getting on remarkably well in her studies with Frank. Whatever either of that gifted pair chose to dispense for his benefit, he received with unenvious admiration.

That year the buzzards drooped low and lower over Tierra Longa. Under the morning haze every hillock, every dying rump was black with them. The fences had been cut and all the cattle turned out to the bone-dry land. Mere crates of bones themselves, they tottered in the trails; they lay down at last with their heads pointed toward the course of the vanished streams, while the buzzards walked solemnly about and made occasional hoarse comments on the ripeness of their condition. The sheep fared better. They could be herded and restrained to their meager allowance of sapless, sun-dried grass. All up the camisal there were lacunae, little natural clearings where only the deer had penetrated before,— *potreros* they were called,—which were opened up for the Palomitas flocks. Peters would cut lanes in the camise, and Kenneth would follow along the sharp stubble with the sheep. It was easier for him than for the men; he could creep in between the thick, interlacing stems and bring back the hunger-driven stragglers.

As they worked up the Torr' there was much of the high-growing chaparral of which the sheep could eat both leaves and bark, and tufts of bunch grass growing in the crevices of the rocks. It was hot, heart-breaking work. Days when they fed close to the Palomitas fence Kenneth would see the gaunt cattle watching them over the wires from their own gnawed pastures. There was something terrifying to the boy in the slender, pointed horns measuring his full length from tip to tip, and the famished eyes underneath. Although Peters reproved him for it, he could not forbear at times to push branches of the buckthorn under the fence. Nights after would often find him running down interminable close lanes of chaparral pursued by formless heads all slender horn and glazing, hungry eyes. Sometimes he would spy his mother at the end of the run and manage to cry out to her, then he would find her comforting him in his bed. Afterward he would hear voices, quarreling, it seemed, but he could never make out over what.

"You'll kill the boy, too, before you're done...What is this place to you that you should sacrifice everything to it? What is it to any of us? There isn't even a living! Just a selfish craze you've got. I'll be glad if they do foreclose. I'll be *glad!* Do you understand? It's taken fifteen years of my life, but I'll not stay until it takes my children!"

"It" was no doubt the terror which pursued him down the blind lanes of sleep. Even his mother was afraid of it.

After Frank joined his father in San Francisco and Mrs. Burke had taken Virginia and the twins away with her to Santa Barbara, Anne used to come out to him in the long afternoons as often as her mother would let her, which was oftener than would have been permitted if she had not—O clever Anne!—thought of bringing her books along with the avowed intention of keeping Kenneth up with his studies. So they made sand maps for geography and learned by heart the "Book of Golden Deeds." The sun turned in his course and the days fell cooler; people began to look prayerfully for the winter rains.

In September they began cutting the post oaks to get at the moss that clung like film to the lower branches.

Burke came over from Agua Caliente that day to offer the consolation of company. Very little passed between the two men beyond a prolonged handshake.

"I'm thinkin' the rain can't hold off much longer," Burke proposed as a likely topic.

Brent turned his hands outward with a gesture that said that any time now would be too long for him. He was a slighter man than his neighbor, but with a sort of personal sureness before which Cornelius, with all Brent's informality, felt often at a disadvantage.

"And yet,"—Brent returned to a subject that was always in his mind,—"there's water...there's thousands of cubic inches of water..." His gaze wandering down the glittering hieroglyphic of the river completed the suggestion. "There's people, too, if they could only get together—why can't they get together?"

"And if they could, the whole bilin' of them wouldn't be the match of the Old Man."

"Ah, but why can't we get together *with* him,—why shouldn't all of our interests be identical? They *are* as a matter of fact; what I can't understand is why a man of Rickart's intelligence don't see it."

"Now, Brent, what for running mate would the lot of *them*"— Burke thrust out his hand toward the cluster of small ranches around Arroyo Verde—"be for the Old Man? There's that to think of."

"We're not so dull as that comes to." A glow began to come into Brent's pale face. "We have ideas,—I have ideas…There's no sense in our having times like this. There's water there…water goin' to waste …and stock dying for want of what the water would grow. Ah, look at it, Burke." Far down they could see the pale gleam of the mud flats in the tulares. "Thousands of cubic feet going to waste every year."

"Well, this is the way I look at it, Misther Brent; there's ideas goin' around loose, slathers of ideas, but the thing that counts is puttin' 'em through. I don't know what quality the Old Man's ideas are, but he gets 'em *through*."

"Oh—through—where? Ahead of the others, perhaps, but where? Your cattle are dying on your hand like flies, Burke. What can even Rickart do when the land turns against us? It takes all of us to fight that, but we are busy fighting one another. And the beasts die—starve—on our hands. We that took them out of their native state and taught them to depend on our care! Ours! You'll save—how many, Burke?"

"One in ten if we're lucky."

"And I—now…" He held up his four fingers; after some consideration he added the thumb to them. "I can hold out five weeks. If the rain doesn't come by then, I shan't save any of them."

"The Old Man is sending me ten tons of alfalfa for the brood stock; I could spare you a couple if it's any help to you," Burke offered.

"Thank you kindly, Cornelius." Brent laughed again his short, light laugh, like a man quite at the bottom of things, secure only in the certainty that nothing worse could happen to him. "I think I ought to tell you that I couldn't pay for it. I'm done, Burke. Morrow wants to foreclose."

"But, man, it's not half the value of the land!"

"That's why. Any other year but this I could raise the money anywhere." They looked quietly out at the shapely, sunny valley with the river winding down. "My wife's not been happy here either," Brent added as the last drop in the cup.

"'T is a hard country for women," Burke conceded. "Men love it, just, but women—they want different things. You've heard," he hinted, "that Rickart is sending me to Summerfield?" Brent nodded. "There's chances there, I'm told, for the pickin'. Maybe now—" Some deeper sympathy than words allowed prevented him from finishing.

Brent got up abruptly and walked to the edge of the veranda.

"That's it," he cried; "that's just it! Wherever the land flings us a handful of coin we run and scramble for it like beggars in the street. And she laughs—she laughs. I tell you, Burke, we've got to master her—we've got to compel her..."

Foreshadowed thus in the talk of their elders, the Brent children felt the approach of disaster. The Burkes added something to that the day they came over to say good-bye; for Cornelius was being transferred to Summerfield to have charge of Rickart's oil interests. Frank was leaving soon for the school for which his tutor had been fitting him. There was a sobering realization of change stilling the impulse of play, as they made for the last time the round of Palomitas. There were a good many pitiful little starved corpses in the camisal, and the air was black with buzzards.

At Mariposa the Ford was bone-white with drought.

"What fun we used to have here when we were little," Virginia sighed. It seemed to them that these things all happened a long time ago. "Oh, well, we'll soon all be together again. My father said so."

"What did he say?" demanded Anne with interest.

"He said if Jevens would give ten thousand more than the mortgage, your father would jump at it."

This was so far from being clear to Kenneth that he took the first opportunity to talk it over with Peters, who told him that it meant

that Jevens was trying to buy Palomitas. Peters was a raw, red-look-
ing man, with absurd yellowish hair sprouting about his crown and
on his upper lip. He had the strength of a steer and not more than
two or three motives, one of which, though he would have denied
it, was a deep, sentimentalized attachment to his employer.

"But my father wouldn't let him have it—he wouldn't," Kenneth
scoffed.

"Oh, well,"—Peters was judicial,—"your paw's a smart man. A
mighty smart man. I ain't much on this oil stock they talk about;
got all the stock I kin tend to right here on Palomitas...kind o' stock
'at keeps itself above ground's all *I* kin tend to." It was Peters's one
joke and he made the most of it.

"Hank Sturgis said the oil stock was going up; right up." Kenneth
did not know what this meant exactly, though he heard it often
enough; he was grateful to Peters for treating him to grown-up conversation.

"Oh, well, now,"—Peters reached out with his bill-hook—there
were bright freckles as large as ten-cent pieces on his raw wrists, and
tufts of reddish hair at the base of his fingers,—"it stands to reason
that they don't know *how* it's going. But your Paw's a master hand
with stock, an' *if* he thinks it's better 'n any stock he's got right here
on Palomitas, you ain't no call to worry none."

It was about this time that Jevens came back. Kenneth, bringing
up the straggling lamb-band that they might have the first go at the
long moss on the fallen oaks, saw him stalking Steven Brent across
the fields, and a little shiver went over him as though Jevens might
have been, what 'Nacio insisted on calling him, *El diablo negro.* But
in the valley everybody was frankly glad to see Mr. Jevens.

To Arroyo Verde, where cattle men, with something in their eyes
strangely like the look of the famished herds, sat about idly under
the wide old sycamores and listened to the dropping of ripe fruit in
the orchards round, Jevens was the incontestable evidence of places
where, and occasions by which the normal procedure of life was
still going on. "Over beyond," which was, in Tierra Longa, a gener-
ic name for the country beyond the Saltillo hills, there was still
money clinking down the arteries of trade; it clinked revivifyingly
for them in Mr. Jevens's pockets. Whatever happened to Tierra

Longa there was still good money to be made in oil.

Those who had been so fortunate as to "get in with the Old Man" held on to all that the relation implied as the drowning to a rope. They took to hope as though it had been to hard drink. They tucked up their feet and let the drought go by them.

On the evening of his return Jevens supped at Palomitas, and addressed most of his conversation to Mrs. Brent, retailing incidents of his trip "over west a ways."

"But I didn't," he remarked, cooling his coffee in his saucer and supporting himself with his elbows on the table, "find just the property I was looking for. I don't know as I see anything which stuck in my eye like this little property right here." It must have been in the cast eye it stuck, for there was nothing that Kenneth could make out, in the one turned toward him, but a velvety, opaque blackness. "I don't know," he repeated, "as I ever see a property which stuck in my eye the way this does."

***

Kenneth heard his mother crying in the room that night. She cried with exasperation and hopeless hurt, and at times with a strange terror. It seemed a part of something that had been going on a long time, as if he might have heard it many nights before and only now taken note of it.

"But there ought to be *something* you could do. There is always *something*." Her voice rose out of sobbing. "After all we've wasted here...time and money...to have to be *turned* out. And it isn't as if you hadn't had an offer, as if you couldn't have gone on your own terms..."

"It wasn't really an offer," he could hear his father answer in a toneless patience; "we don't know that we'd have gotten out with anything in that case either. We could pull through if we had rain—just one good rain—God!" He broke off with the same note of bitter helplessness.

"It isn't *going* to rain...Why would Mr. Rickart send the Burkes away if he thought it would rain? If a man like that gives up, what's the sense of *your* holding on!"

"He isn't giving up. It's only that he's learned that he must have a bigger man, more scientific management. He's sending Burke to Summerfield to let him down easy."

"He'll make his fortune for him first, anyway…"

There was a silence in which Kenneth dropped almost into the pit of dreams. Suddenly the trouble broke out again with a torturing, impatient cry.

"Oh—you are going to *sleep!* You can sleep! And you don't know if the children and I are to have a roof over our heads! No wonder things go on the way they do when you don't have it on your mind any more than *that!*"

Kenneth sat up in bed struggling with his stupor; he was under the impression that this was addressed somehow to himself. Then he heard the trouble die away in dull sobbing and protesting, extenuating endearment. It mingled with the voices that pursued him down the labyrinths of drought and sleep…

from *Chapter V*

It wasn't in the least, as Anne had said, like an artesian well. It came up from the pumps in black, pasty gobs, and stank. That was Kenneth's first impression of the oil fields the November evening that Peters drove them down to Summerfield with their goods lumbering behind them in the wool wagon. They lay, the half-hundred wells, in the hollow of an old earthquake drop that took a curving line about the town and left it high on the up-tilted side. At the foot of the drop the waste of the river seeped away and the hollow climbed by degrees to the comb of the mesa, drawn all in fine puckers where the flocks had left it bare to the ruining rains. In the early dusk they made out the derricks each by his little, danger-red eye, like half-formed, prehistoric creatures feeling their way up from the depths to light, leaning all together with the slight undulations of the land, and seeming to communicate in low, guttering blubs and endless creakings, as though they plotted to tear loose at any moment and stamp out the little hordes of men who ran perpetually about, or collected in knots among the sheds with their heads together.

There were crowds of men. The night the Brents had driven up, belated, to the hotel, they saw them standing weariedly about the bar like storks, puffy with want of sleep, and yet always with a tense, waiting air. Rows of men slumped in chairs in the dim-lit halls, trying to sleep, and outside in the street men walked up and down as though no such thing as sleep were thought of....

"They're shooting a well over at the Escondita; we can just make it..."

So a peace was patched up which carried them over the week-end to Virginia's Sunday party which was to mark the farewell of the

Burkes to Petrolia. Virginia's faculty for making an occasion of everything carried them to such a pitch of entertainment that it was not until Kenneth was well on his way home that he discovered that all the hollow had been retaken by one of the thick white fogs which at this season haunted the boundaries of ancient waters. Feeling his way home through the ghastly murk, Kenneth became aware, by striking his shins against it, that he had passed east of his proper path and come up against one of the great pipes that led to the reservoirs on the hill. He thought, however, that if he felt along it he should presently come to a cross-line by which he could trace his way back to the trail. He trotted along, hoping for a clue, liking the quiet of the night and the palpable smother of the fog which had swept all the day's warmth into the hollow before it. Finally the slope of the ground warned him that he must have struck above rather than below the cross-line. He had hardly appreciated this discovery until he came out quite unexpectedly on the rise of the land above the wells, and found himself clear of fog. It lay all below him, woolly white under a watery moon, heaving a little and faintly splashed here and there with derrick lights. All about the rim the reservoirs clung like great ticks sucking the black juices of the land, bloated with it to bursting. The pitch of the corrugated roofs and the open vents gave them a deliberative air, as though they calculated, with a slow, leech-like intelligence, where next to strike. The boy was not afraid of the night nor of the hills behind him, drawing into deep, velvety folds under the moon, but he was afraid suddenly of that mysterious quality taken on by the works of man, power ungoverned by sensibility. The fog, which lay level with the rim of the hollow, shook and billowed as though the thing under it which men had made had grown suddenly too big for them and was stirring in its own control.

It stirred and turned upon itself and released a strange, many-limbed creature that, in the instant of hair-raising horror, while he looked, wormed its way up the roof of the nearest tank, the upper side of which was almost level with the ground. The fog cleared into the moonlight, however, and enabled him to distinguish the figures of two men that wrestled and broke apart and clutched again in a heavy, breathing intensity unbroken by any other sound.

He had hardly grasped the situation, had not freed it from the start and shock of the supernatural in which it seemed to have begun, by the time the two figures had worked over half the space of the thin iron roof toward the open vent. There was an opening in every tank, left so for the escape of gases that gathered above the oil under the steady sun, and it occurred to Kenneth that one of the men might have been the watchman closing the tanks against the chance of rain. If it had been the purpose of the second man to prevent him, he was making no headway in the terrible, keen wrestle which carried them every moment nearer the vent. It was in the instant that they rocked together on the very edge of it that Kenneth's recognition of the danger burst from him in a cry, shrilled by his own recent shock of ghostly fear. It caught the wrestlers in mid-clutch, and with the start and the loosening hold the figure which had been pressing the other toward the rim of the vent, sprang backward, gave a swift, running leap and plunged into the crawling smother of the fog not ten feet away from where Kenneth stood. He had instinctively shut his eyes in the crisis of his astonishment, and when he opened them the second figure was nowhere to be seen. For a moment he stared at the empty roof, ribbed in thin lines of light and shadow by the watery moon. Then suddenly a horrible thing arose upon him from the vent; black and glistening with its native slime it crawled blindly out and toward him, shaking its unrecognizable head and pawing at it with slimy, shapeless hands. The unexpectedness of the apparition, falling in with all his secret thought about the wells and the strange, unearthly life of the derricks, was stronger than the obvious explanation.

With a sharp sob of terror, Kenneth turned and plunged into the friendly cover of the fog. He ran a long time blindly, falling and rising to run again without pausing to take note of his direction, until, by the process of stumbling over them, he had accounted for the most familiar of the iron ribs that held the place together. Once the accustomed touch of the Escondita pipes had restored him, his feet carried him almost unconsciously in the direction of a yellow smear issuing from the opened doors and windows of a house that, as he approached it, swelled out upon him suddenly, full of running figures and low, excited noises. He saw them pass and repass the

blurred squares of the windows and then one, touched with a certain familiarity, leaped out through the wedge of an opened door
and was swallowed up by the fog. It was a full minute before he realized that the house was his own home and the figure Peters. It was
some minutes more before he fairly recovered his wits; then sus-
pecting that the stir and the anxiety might be on his account, for he
had no notion how long he had been blundering about in the fog,
he went briskly up the back steps where the light on that side of the
house was brightest.

"H—ssh!" Addie warned him; she was nursing a kettle of water
over the fire newly kindled. "Where's Anne?"

He was answering her in a usual tone, for the arrangement had
been perfectly aboveboard that his sister was to stay the night with
Virginia, and he resented the implication of her caution; but
"Hush!" she said again. She was listening, strained and anxiously
toward the living-room, where now he could make out the figure of
a Summerfield doctor and a woman in a nurse's dress who came to
the doctor's side for a moment and disappeared again in his mother's room.

"Mis' Brent's took bad," Addie told him; he caught the degree of
seriousness from her use of the title. Ordinarily Addie referred to
her mistress as "your ma."

"Where's my father?"

"In there." The jerk of Addie's head, as she blew the flame, was
toward the door of his mother's room, made all at once mysterious,
unenterable.

Kenneth wandered into the living-room where presently, as the
doctor and the nurse consulted together in low tones, he thought
they must have mentioned him.

"He'd better go to bed," he heard the doctor say; but no one spoke
to him nor asked where he had been so long. In his own room at
last, he began to undress, but the wall between it and his mother's
room was thin; sounds came through to him, unbearable. He sat
there on the edge of his bed with his hands over his ears.

from *Cactus Thorn*

Chapter 1

Arliss had made two or three turns about the station platform before he saw her. Scarcely then, so drugged his gaze by the naked glare of a land whose very shadows looked rusted by the sun, could he take her in, lovely as she was, as a separate item of the landscape. She must have been sitting just there in the shelter of the alfalfa bales, when the construction train had dropped him a quarter of an hour ago, taking him in with that same wide gaze, incurious as an animal's, which dropped without a spark as it crossed his own.

Arliss had been two days laying the raw silences of the desert to his soul. Not too long for him to be struck with the quality of her detachment, but long enough for him to put it to himself that the astonishing thing was, not that he had found a young and beautiful woman there, but having found her, she did not disturb for him the somnolent desert charm. She was less of an item in it than the dwindling hoot of the train from whose caboose he had just descended, or the slinking rails over which, sometime that afternoon, the belated Flier would pick him up again.

He passed her the second time, to find that by some slight shift of her personality she had contrived, as some wild thing might, to remove herself even further from the scant field of his attention. But in the very moment of recognizing this removal he found himself yielding again to the pressure of vacuity which held him to the contemplation of the land's empty reach, its disordered horizons, its vast, sucking stillness.

It was to secure for himself just this long, uninterrupted wait at the ramshackle station from whose high platform ores had once been shipped to forgotten smelters, that he had used his name, not unknown even so far from New York, to have himself dropped there to await the belated Flier from the east.

What he found in the untenanted valley, rising far on either side into nameless, broken ranges, was so exactly the reflection of his inward state that he was able, in his pacing rounds, to forget the presence of the girl until the high wheeling sun drove him automatically to shelter. The stir she made, making room for him in the only possible seat among the miscellaneous crates and bales, brought to him afresh not only the singularity of her being there, in a situation which could not be supposed to be improved by the presence of an unknown man, but the greater singularity of his not being in the least affected by her. There was a queer tug of conventionality within him, and a queerer drop in recognition of his failure to respond to any suggestion that might lie in her beauty and their aloneness; beauty of the same sleepy smoothness as the land itself, isolation subject only to the interruption of the Flier three or four hours hence.

And yet, for all effect she had upon him, she might, like the horned lizard starting from under his foot, have assembled herself from the tawny earth and the hot sand, or at a word resolve herself into the local element.

So absolute was this sense of her being a part of the place and the day, that it was with the effect of going on with a suspended conversation that she presently addressed him.

"I wouldn't, if I were you," she suggested queerly, "not unless you are used to it." Forgetting why he had sat down, Arliss had made a restless movement to resume his pacing. To hide the start she gave him, he squinted upward toward the hot, shallow heaven.

"Isn't it safe?" he wished to know.

"Over in Pahwahnit," she said, with vague pointing movements of her throat and chin, "days like this, men drop dead with water in their canteens." Arliss remembered to have heard this.

"I didn't know Pahwahnit was so near." He looked with interest toward that one of the low, mottled ranges which the girl had indicated.

"Oh, *near!*" she smiled. "It would be a good horse would take you to Pahwahnit in three days, from here. And your friends might be a month finding you."

"Ah," he became whimsical in turn, "that would suit me!" She gave him a moment of grave appreciation:

"It sure is a good country to lose yourself in."

Arliss reflected that this might well be a preliminary to finding yourself, which was what he had come west to do.

"The point being, of course," he said, "that there should be people interested in looking for you."

She considered this literally. "There's a ranch at Bennet Wells," she enumerated, "and two men doing assessment at the Bonnie Bell. Then there's always likely to be vaqueros. And the Indians. Only the Indians wouldn't know you were lost unless you told them. They would think you were simply taking a *paseo.*"

"Ah, then," Arliss insisted, "there *are* people who manage to live here."

"Oh, live! If you can call it that!" she flashed at him. "People don't really live here: they just happen along and stay." She seemed to keep pace silently with his thought which made a backward cast toward ancient uses of the desert. "Of course," she began again, "if you've got something to think out—" and then at his quick recognition of the personal touch, by the same subtle means which he had sensed earlier, she momentarily withdrew herself. Arliss felt himself remanded to the traveller's impersonal claim for information.

"I mean, would it be possible to get food and housing for a few months, while you *are* thinking it out?"

She nodded. "There's a sort of a town between those two ranges that look so close together; and ranches scattered about. It's a question really of water. When you have water you can have anything you want. *Any*thing!" She appeared to measure him a moment before selecting the confirming incident. "There was a man had an Italian villa here once. Over there, at Hawainda."

Arliss could just make it out, a scar on the furthest range where the crude reds and ochers of the plain altered subtly to pearl and amethyst, and the rusty shadows began to creep from under the heavy glare, and to fill the passes with blue drift.

"They say the very stones were brought from Italy, and marble seats and fountains for the terraced gardens, packed in by mule backs—that was the story."

"There would be a story," Arliss agreed, "and a woman." It was the first note of sophistication he had ventured, and her low amused laugh was the measure of her response.

"Three of them," she agreed. "His wife and two daughters. *They* had had about all they could stand of the desert when Beasley struck it rich; and he built the villa after they had been a year in Italy. He couldn't imagine what else it was they wanted. There's been no one there for years now, except Indians. They wouldn't live in the house, of course; they're superstitious. But they keep up the water pipes and the reservoir, I've heard, so they can play with the fountains."

"Oh, not really! Everybody *told* me I should find romance in the west, but I hadn't expected anything so good as this."

"Is that what you call romantic?" The girl frowned slightly to herself. "The Beasley women hated it, I've heard. They didn't lose any time getting out of it when the old man died. I suppose," she considered, "a thing can't seem romantic when it's the only thing that ever happened to you...there must be plenty of empty houses in New York that aren't in the least romantic."

"Ah," cried Arliss, caught, "how did you know I am from New York?" and immediately perceived that he had touched too nearly on that instinct by which, like some delicate insect, she took a sudden color of aloofness from the soil.

"There's a lot of easterners out here every year," she let fall from behind the veil; "we get so we can pretty generally tell where they come from."

The check, if it amounted to that, was one that Arliss refused to admit, all the more because of the implied fatuousness of his momentary hope that she might have recognized him. It wasn't unlikely; he had many followers in the west and his picture was one of the stock cuts of contemporary news. But he was not so fatuous as not to feel, in the moment of perceiving himself still unknown, a measure of the freedom he had come so far to find. He returned, as far as possible, to the note of detachment in his next question.

"And just where *have* we come? Where am I now, in respect to places one hears of—Los Angeles, for instance? And how would I go to that place—where the villa is?"

"Hah-wah-eenda," she pronounced with the soft southern roll. "It's an Indian word for Place of the Doves. There was always water there, and they built their nests—You'd have to go by train from Loos Ahng-lace," again she gave him the soft, informing drawl, "to Barstow, I guess, and from there to Minietta, it's two days by pack train, and then north across the long arm of Mesquite..." But already Arliss' interest had dropped. By the very vastness which her use of names and distances implied, he was beguiled again into that vacuity of mind which in his present situation of spiritual exhaustion, appeared to him as the happiest state.

After a perfunctory question or two he found himself, this time unwarned, resuming his aimless round, and by a vague impulse of propriety, extending it down the track and around the point of an ancient lava flow, temporarily out of sight and sound of his fellow islander. Here, for an hour he so successfully maintained his wished for detachment, that until he came in sight of her again he was hardly aware that he had turned his steps back toward the station shed. She had risen and was moving about with a familiar definiteness which, by aid of a white napkin spread upon a bale of hay, and the inward prompting which had turned him back upon his path, he recognized as meal getting.

Arliss had made no provision for himself during the long hours which must elapse before he could reach the dining car of the Flier, and the way in which she had taken this for granted in laying places for two at her improvised table, struck him as one more item in the complete identification of the young woman with the place and the day. In a country in which the whole machinery of impulse and foresight is sucked out of a man, it is natural that food should simply appear.

She had produced, doubtless from some place where they were stored for just such emergencies, the simplest of equipments for making tea, and only waited for him to fetch water for it from the near-by tank, to include him in her arrangements.

"Your train may be late, you know," she had opposed to his

conventional hesitancy over her proffered hospitality. It aroused him for the first time, by the implication of its not being her train also, to the question, since it was not to take the only possible train, what in the name of desolation she was there for? Not venturing to ask, he filled the extemporized kettle and placed it over the fire she had kindled amid the aimless wheel tracks at the back of the station.

It was a little past noon of the clock, that magical moment when the shadows begin to stir and crouch for their evening assault upon the plain, and the burnt reds, and the thick yellows and pale ash of the desert, clear and flash into translucent flame. In such moments one perceives the lure of the desert to be the secret lure of fire, to which in rare moments men have given themselves as to a goddess. While it lasted it seemed to Arliss that the whole land leaped alive from the kindling of their wayfaring hearth. It leaped subtly almost to the surfaces of this pale brown girl, as if she were, like the land, but the outward sheath of incredible hot forces that licked him with elusive tips before they dropped to the crackle of twigs under the kettle on the bare sand. Turning to gather a handful of fuel, he found the thin flame-colored film of the cactus flower almost under his fingers. Before the girl's sharp deterring exclamation reached him, he drew back his inexperienced hand, wounded with the cactus thorn.

"There's only one way to admire a cactus," she commiserated, and while he fumbled for his handkerchief to swathe his pricked fingers, she held up the delicate blossom on the point of a small dagger which she had produced unobtrusively from somewhere about her person.

"I didn't know that the thorns simply jumped at you like that," Arliss apologized, taking the proffered dagger, not so much to admire the sun rayed flower as to wonder at the implement on which it was impaled. It was slender like a thorn, and had a carved ivory handle which had been broken and mended deftly with bone. He wondered where she carried it and what provocation would have brought it leaping against himself.

"I suppose," he said gravely, handing it back to her, "that this is a typical desert experience; to admire and be stung."

The girl laughed, laying the flower back in the shade of its parent leaf and half consciously heaping a little sand over the severed end of the stem. "The desert's got a worse name than it deserves," she defended; "there's ways it has to be lived with…I suppose you'd be just as likely to be killed crossing Fifth Avenue if you didn't know the rules."

"Well," he admitted, "New York can sting you to death, too. But one reads—all sorts of things about how the desert lays hold on a man and never lets go."

"Oh, yes, it gets them. It seems to *want* people." She considered the wide untenanted spaces, the rich promise of the soil. "It wants them too much," she concluded. "It is like a woman, you know—that has only one man or child: she loves it to death."

"That," said Arliss, "is positively the most alarming thing I have heard about it." She seriously agreed.

"There's accidents, of course, like missing the trail or getting out of water. But they are likely to happen to you anywhere. The desert sort of sucks you empty and throws you away. That is, unless you are willing to take what it gives you in place of what you had."

"Then it does give you something?"

"Everything!" she averred. "only…you can't pick and choose." She turned back to an earlier phase of their conversation. "If you had come here to think something out, you know. Well, you won't."

"Won't think?"

"It will be done for you. Like a piece of knitting that you've got all wrong. It's taken out of your hands and unraveled; all you have to do is watch it being set right."

"Then I have come to exactly the right place!" He tried for the note of lightness to cover a certain dismay. For the one thing he knew he hadn't come for was to have things taken any more completely out of his hands. It was, he himself would have said, to get his thinking thoroughly in hand again, to restore his lost sense of ascendency over a situation which, for the moment, impressed him as having points in common with the trackless land whose horizons were lost in illimitable disordered ranges.

He was sitting on the bare sand beside his companion, who for the purpose of tending their kettle, had dropped there with a lithe unconsciousness of habit. The homely occupation gave him a more direct sense of her personality than he had yet received. More a woman than a girl, he decided—twenty-three or four, perhaps— but of her experience nothing could be judged. There was nothing western about her as he had learned to recognize westernness in current fiction. Her dress, the hat and the jacket of which she had laid aside, was such as the more competent of city stenographers might have worn.

But even while he speculated, she had turned from him in one of those lovely poses the secret of which was known only to the early Greeks, and poked at a greyish spot of earth with a stick. It looked a little firmer, perhaps, than the surrounding sand. Then to his amazement, the spot gathered itself together and scurried off toward the shelter of the cactus thorns. For a moment the spiked, squat head was held alert, the broad body pulsating with startled life, quieting slowly as the little creature dropped back upon its belly, and with a slight burrowing motion became again a part of the sun and shade mottled sand.

"I guess they have the right of it," the girl commented with one of those occasional odd lapses into colloquialism which Arliss had already speculated over. "They never start any knitting of their own. They take it all out in making themselves a part of the big pattern." She dropped the stick, and with a beautiful half turn toward the open country, took the measure of its vastness in her speech. "That's the best thing you get out of the desert. It teaches you never to make anything up. Like...," this time she searched the wide earth for comparison, "like marriage is with us."

This was the sort of thing that, said in the circle to which Arliss was accustomed, would have cleared instantly for the speaker an advanced position on the Freudian premise. It should have led, by way of "complexes" and a discussion of the Russian realists, to precisely the breath-shortening crisis from which it was supposed to tear the veil.

Said as a preliminary to the announcement that the kettle had boiled, it had the effect of one of those inadvertent gestures by which in the middle of the game, the board is suddenly cleared. It left the other member of the engagement with hand extended and no piece to play.

Without waiting for an answer, apparently without expecting any, she took up the kettle and leading the way back to their improvised table, gave herself to the administration of hospitality and the simple enjoyment of the meal. On her feet and moving she was even more beautiful than Arliss had at first conceded, and less provocative, an effect that was heightened by the girl's failure to make of the primitive ritual of fire and food, man and woman in the wilderness, the note of sex appeal. Evidently she found nothing in their situation to inhibit this casual introduction of a topic they were both young enough to approach with trepidation. He had to admit to himself, however, if any such trepidation existed on her part, it was admirably concealed. He found himself under the necessity of reviving the topic himself, if he was to discover what, if anything, she had meant by it.

"So you think," he suggested, "that marriage is made up."

"On one side or the other," she agreed. "I have seen the wild creatures mating, and I've never seen them unhappy in it. But I've seldom seen humans where one or both of them wasn't suffering, because they had already made up their minds beforehand that marriage ought to be something it hadn't turned out to be with them. That's what I mean about the effect that the desert has on men. If you come into it with your mind made up as to what you want to get from it, you may not get anything."

"But," Arliss expostulated, "when we go after anything we have to begin where we are."

"No," she shook her head thoughtfully. "You have to begin where *It* is. Like I said with marriage. You have to begin with what loving is, and cut your marriage accordingly. It's like match and a piece of wood. After they come together you can't treat them any more as wood and match, but as fire, and deal with them according to the nature of fire."

"And if the fire goes out?" Arliss had that instinctive fear of the irrecoverable nature of marriage which manifests as a covert curiosity.

He was still far from admitting that his fear was the obverse side of an incapacity so far to make the whole hearted approach, but he had begun to wonder whether the mystery of his waning appetite for leadership, his reluctance to accept the opportunity held out to him, for fear his interest in its exercise might not hold out, were not of the same nature as the evanescent flame of passion. With that uncanny prescience for the trend of his secret thought which he had already noted in this singular young woman, his companion pointed her contempt with a glance at the burnt ends of sticks from which the flame of their own fire had already receded.

"There's ways of handling fire," she said. "You can spend all your time keeping it going, or you can build it up fresh when you need it from the coals. That's what I meant by being made up, when it ought to be something that exists, that is there all the time, like a well, or…" she reverted to the earlier figure, "like a fire in the depths of the earth, or fire in the sun. You oughtn't to have to keep poking at it to make it burn."

"Ah," he said, "I thought it was the business of women in particular to keep the fire burning…priestesses of the flame." She took him in again with that incurious animal like gaze. "You would," she said, with an impersonal finality that made Arliss aware that, though he had never so stated it to himself, that was exactly what he had long wished to think. He knew that he had been thinking of marriage for himself as a possible way out of his present state of spiritual insufficiency. If only he could find a woman who could be counted on to kindle a flame and keep it going, he might at that glow, warm the slowly chilling reaches of his intellect and his ambition. He had also a momentary panic lest this strange young woman, in placing him so accurately on one point had not also penetrated to the place of the chill and discovered what he had left New York to hide. Before he could, however, frame any sort of an answer to this pointed judgment of himself, his companion had flicked the personal element from it with the shaking out of the crumbs of their meal, and was going on with her own thought. "I suppose," she half mused, "that's one of the ways in which women got sidetracked. They didn't *have* to keep making up the fire all the time, the way men do. They *lived* in the flame, until men got to think of them as being makers of the flame…" She dropped off with such complete disregard of her companion that for a moment he failed to follow her into simple comment on the country, the climate, the trails that went white and blind across the baked land.

Arliss was conscious of a vague irritation with this singular young person who "talked sex"—that was the way it was phrased in Arliss' own circle—and dropped it in that calm way just as the man was beginning to get interested. He would have liked to keep on with the subject, to point his protest against her reading on the function of woman, as priestess of the flame, by his own need to feel the flame, any flame, for just the kindling touch which he was beginning to feel she might have given, and so negligently refused. Here were all the materials of fire, the romantic setting, the woman with her satisfying contours, the shadows of her hair like rusted gold, the fruity brownness of her skin. Where he had been astonished that she did not move him more at the beginning of their acquaintance, he found himself vexed in the discovery that her mind was not even on the business of whether she moved him or not. His annoyance, however, was not deep enough to be proof against the simple charm of her talk, friendly and impersonal as a boy's, charged with all a boy's interest and information of the region in which they found themselves marooned. Gradually his mind loosened its tension and ran out happily on the track which her talk provided. At the end of an hour he was startled by the wild hooting of his approaching train in the narrow cañon to their right.

The girl stood up, beginning to assemble her belongings with instinctive feminine movements of setting herself to rights. Arliss rose also, and for want of anything else to say, expressed the conventional hope that they were continuing their journey together.

"Oh, no!" she told him; she was expecting friends who would come for her;—she threw a casual glance back toward the encircling hills and took the position of the sun,—in another hour, she said. And as she stood serene in her utter lack of any need of him, that happened which by every calculation of social incidence should have happened in the beginning. As at the striking of a match Arliss felt himself swept suddenly by the need of her, the need of a man for a woman, as natural as the need of water and as necessary as bread. She stood buttoning her ready jacket which fitted her lovely curves as it might have fitted the Bronze Diana pointing her perpetual arrow within view of Arliss' New York office. Her brown eyes, pale brown like the shadows under the sage, smiled at him with the first glint of natural coquetry.

"I've been very happy to meet you, Mr. Arliss," she said.

"Ah," he cried, "I didn't tell you that!"

"Well, couldn't I just have seen your picture in the papers?...it's there often enough."

There was so little to say to this that for the moment that was left to them amid the approaching thunder Arliss let his glance roam over her hungrily, until in passage it crossed her own for an instant in which she took the measure of his desire and disallowed it, as the cool surface of a statue might for a moment reflect without being warmed by it, a passing torch. She clasped the hand which he formally held out to her, and shook it gravely. "Good-bye," she said, and again, "I'm very glad to have met you!"

from "George Sterling
at Carmel"

from *"George Sterling at Carmel"*

Strange now to recall that the thing most worth recalling of the early years of 1900 was the rumor of a new poet of Keatsian promise, rising somewhere about the Golden Gate—Oakland, was it, or Piedmont, or San Francisco? Searching all the horizons of print one discovered that his name was Sterling, and that his Keatsian flavor was neither imitative nor too pronounced. In 1903 I published a book about the Land of Little Rain where I was then living, and received a note from Sterling which proved him generous, shy and discriminating. A year later I met him.

That Summer of 1904 I had gone down to Old Monterey to study what was left of Spanish California backgrounds, for a novel. Returning to San Francisco, I was reported in the daily press as being entranced with the locality to the point of determining some day to have a home there. Thus notified of my presence in his neighborhood, promptly arrived George Sterling, whose first personal remark was that he, too, meant to settle somewhere about Carmel Bay, with no more delay than the building preliminaries called for. Sterling and Henry Laffler, the literary editor of the *Argonaut*, called together, for Laffler at that time, with the sense of its being a tremendously worth-while office, had cast himself for the part of literary impresario to young talent on the Pacific Coast. Sterling was as handsome as a Roman faun, shy, restless, slim and stooping; giving the impression, though we were within a few months of each other as to years, of being entitled to the extenuations of youth, which I, for my part, never denied him. The business of the call was to invite me to dinner at Coppa's.

One dined so well in San Francisco in those days. Such heaping platefuls of fresh shrimp for appetizers! Such abalone chowder, such savory and melting sand-dabs, salads so crisp, vegetables in such profusion, and pies so deep and flaky. Such Dago red, fruity, sharp and warming! And all for thirty-five cents! At Coppa's that night there was also spaget', and, replacing the ubiquitous American pie, little almond crumby tartlets well filled with whipped cream. Beside Laffler and Sterling, there were a short man with the face of a Breton sailor and hair like one of Fra Angelico's angels, who turned out to be James Hopper; a square cropped Aztec glyph whose name was Zavier Martinez; one of the Irwins, I think; and other such students of the creative arts who adventured so gloriously along the coasts of Bohemia.

Coppa's was one of the preferred resorts of such as these. They had decorated it in the manner of art students, with gay, clever and slightly ribald comment and sketch, of which I recall only a fragment of half burned plaster turned up, still smoking a day or two after the San Francisco fire, of a Chestertonian gentleman helping himself generously to pie, to the inscription, "Paste makes Waist." The afternoon following that dinner Sterling walked with me to Portsmouth Square, while I filled the Stevenson galleon with violets. We had tea and cumquats in a neighboring Chinese restaurant, and the poet read me passages from "The Testimony of the Suns." So no more until I met him again at Carmel in the late Summer of 1905.

II

The Mission San Carlos Borromeo looks inshore up the valley of Carmel to the lilac-colored crests of Santa Lucia; off shore, the view just clears the jaws of Lobos along the sunpath between it and Cypress Point. Full in the crescent bay the sea lifts in a hollow curve of chrysoprase, whose edge goes up in smoking foam along the hard packed beaches—ever and ever, disregardful of the nondescript shacks, the redwood bungalows and pseudo-Spanish haciendas crowding one another between the beach and the high road. But when I first came to this land, a virgin thicket of buckthorn sage and sea-blue lilac spread between well-spaced, long-leaved pines. The dunes glistened white with violet shadows, and in warm hollows, between live oaks, the wine of light had mellowed undisturbed a thousand years.

Sterling's first choice was the delectable point at the turn of the road toward Sur, on the Carmel side of Harry Leon Wilson's "Ocean Home," giving directly upon the sea. This proving too far from the final town site, he built at last upon a similar point of pines, all but islanded by meadow, looking toward Santa Lucia and Palo Corona. To reach it from the town one climbed a piney hill, threaded the close encinas, skirting a lovely lake of herd grass all afoam with flowers, and then went along a ravine made secret by dark, leaning bays. James Hopper owned it after Sterling, and afterward it went up in fire, somehow an appropriate end. George was the last man in the world to have wished the house where his happiest years were passed to become a gaping place to the penny curious.

The heart of the Sterling house was a long room overlooking the woodland prospect, with a huge square fireplace at one end, which it was the poet's pride to keep well filled with fat pitch-pine backlogs; but George could seldom be found there by daylight. We achieved, all of us who flocked there within the ensuing two or three years, especially after the fire of 1906 had made San Francisco uninhabitable to the creative worker, a settled habit of morning work, which it was anathema to interrupt. But by the early afternoon mail one and another of the painter and writer folk could be seen sauntering by piney trails, which had not then suffered that metamorphosis of asphalt, concrete and carbon monoxide that go in the world of realtors by the name of "improvements," to sun themselves along the town's one partially cleared passage to the sea, and make delightful impromptu disposals of the rest of the day.

It was the simplest occupations that gave the most pleasure, and yielded the richest harvest of impressions, observations and feeling-response, which are the stuff of the artist life and the envy and hate-edged amazement of the outsider. Sterling's greatest pleasures were those that whetted his incessant appetite for sensation—the sting of the surf against his body, the dangerous pull of the undertow off the Carmel beaches, or gathering seafood among the "undulant, apple-green hollows" of the Mission Cove. He also delighted to go striding, ax on shoulder, over the Monterey hills looking for pitch pine, or for bee-trees, or whatever arduous and practical simplicity restored him to that human touch, from which it was his weakness to fall away, or perhaps never quite to attain in any other relation.

Of all our walks he loved best the one on Point Lobos, no poet's stroll, but a stout climb, dramatic, danger-tipped, in the face of bursting spray-heads torn up from primordial deeps of sea gardens, resolved into whorls and whorls of lambent color. Interrupting or terminating such excursions, there would be tea beside driftwood fires, or mussel roasts by moonlight—or the lot of us would pound abalone for chowder around the open-air grill at Sterling's cabin. And talk—ambrosial, unquotable talk!

How shall one account for the charms of life lived solely for its creative values, a charm that holds over to the mere recital of it, even for those who have never entered into its subtle simplicities? Yet one must account a little to explain why there gathered such a company at Carmel, at the furthest geographical remove from the distributing center for creative work. I had already tasted life in the Latin Quarter of Paris, and at Florence, among the "prairie dogs"— you know, those pensive ladies who sit in cafés with elbows on the table, and paws adroop, propping their chins, and mouths slightly open to receive wisdom—when Gordon Craig was their prophet, and people used to follow Isadora Duncan respectfully in the streets—young Isadora who could dance—merely to enjoy the subtle motions of her walking. I had been entertained at the dingy, eternally hopeful resorts of Soho by English novelists, who had happily survived them, and lived two years in Greenwich Village two floors under Hendrik Willem Van Loon, before he became a best seller, when Jimmy managed the Mad Hatter, coming to rest finally at the foot of Cinco Pintores Hill, where the diversions of creative activity range all the way from dance-drama of the Stone Age to taking tea with John Galsworthy and Sinclair Lewis at the same time. But none of these experiences keeps so fresh a savor as the eight or ten years at Carmel when George Sterling was easily the most arresting figure.

There was beauty and strangeness; beauty of Greek quality, but not too Greek; "green fires, and billows tremulous with light," not wanting the indispensable touch of grief; strangeness of bearded men from Tassajara with bear meat and wild-honey to sell; great teams from the Sur, going by on the highroad with a sound of bells; and shadowy recesses within the wood, white with the dropping of night-haunting birds. But I think that the memorable and now vanished charm of Carmel lay, perhaps, most in the reality of the simplicity attained, a simplicity factually adjusted to the quest of food and fuel and housing as it can never be in any "quarter" of city life. And very much more than we at that time realized, it nearly all derived from George Sterling, between whom and the environment there was a perfection of suitability that mediated for even the clumsiest the coveted level of simplicity.

III

The story of his life happenings is as meager as Hawthorne's or Whittier's. While still a youth he went adventuring to California, but no further than a desk in the office of his uncle, Frank C. Havens, a realtor of importance in the transbay regions of San Francisco. In his twenties he married Caroline Rand, a stenographer in the office where he was clerk. The high points of his own rating were his acquaintance with Ambrose Bierce and Jack London. Bierce, whom he met about the time he began to write, directed his reading, which never quite made up the lack of formal education. If, as the poet admitted, Bierce also formed his taste, it was at least a taste which, left to itself, never faltered to either side of a narrowly classic line.

Never having seen Bierce but once, at Sterling's house, and having known him only through young people who had passed under his hand, I judged him to be a man secretly embittered by failure to achieve direct creation, to which he never confessed; a man of immense provocative power, always secretly—perhaps even to himself—seeking to make good in some other's gift what he himself had missed, always able to forgive any shortcoming in his protégés more easily than a failure to turn out according to his prescription. I thought him something of a posturer, tending to overweigh a slender inspiration with apocalyptic gestures. I am sure he left as many disciples sticking in the bog of unrealized aspiration as ever he drew out on firm ground; but Sterling, who carried loyalty to excess, never faced the precise values of his association with Bierce. Which leads me to suspect that he did not feel altogether sure of their surpassing character. In the end they drifted into an attitude of slightly veiled antagonism over George's acceptance, chiefly on the authority of Jack London, of Jack's version of Socialism.

It was Sterling's humanitarianism which led him in that direction, for he was not really informed on the subject. He was a little touched too, or perhaps it was only his admiration for Jack made it seem so, with London's sense of the importance of the Nordic in the scheme of things. But his true devotion was to beauty, in which he found the supreme reality and the final test of excellence in art— the test, too, of his own personal metal. For no Puritan could more cleanly have excised out of his work all that any hide-bound Puritan would have found unacceptable in his behavior. It was the keenest criticism of his own life, and of our work, that Sterling could have made; all the more biting because he was, I think, quite unconscious of making it.

If George took his sociology from Jack, it was not without recompense. At that time one found him reading manuscript and proof for London with a meticulous interest that never flagged; his diction was irreproachable, and his feeling for the fall of a sentence and the turn of a figure peculiarly sensitive. The two of them used to talk over their literary projects with even exchange. If Jack developed themes of George's originating—for Jack had that pliability of genius which enabled him to work freely in anybody's material— he stinted neither credit nor *kudos*. Moreover, I have always suspected that London's open buying of plots for short stories from any writer with more plots than places to bestow them was chiefly a generous camouflage for help that could not be asked or given otherwise without embarrassment. Jack took an aesthetic pleasure in displaying the open hand, but never, to my knowledge, with the least tinge of patronage.

Nor did Sterling ever withhold anything that one poet could ask of another. I recall once his coming to me to borrow fifty dollars— Jack, usually his banker for such accommodations, being then on the voyage of the *Snark*—not for himself, but to lend to one he judged more necessitous. "But George," I protested, "that man can never say anything bad enough about me; it would be poison to him to take my money." "That's why," explained the poet ingenuously, "if you lend it to me and I lend it to him, he'll never know." George expected generosities like that of other people, and achieved them, too, for, though he had sharp hates and quick resentments, he could never be faithful to them to the extent of doing less than justice—and very often, indeed, a little more than justice—to the other man's work.

IV

Jack London and I had to shake down a bit before we began to get on together. There was the difference in type, for one thing, and the constantly dissolving and reforming ring of Jack's admirers, inclined to resent my being unimpressed by Jack's recent discovery of Darwinian evolution. Nor could I ever take London's pronouncement of the Social Revolution so seriously as did his adorers—and who of the younger set in those days was not an adorer of Jack London? But in time, largely by way of Jack's new wife Charmian, we arrived at a Platonic exchange.

They were to me, these two—Jack and George—the first professional literary men that I had known, a source of endless intellectual curiosity. They were, for example, the first people I had known who could get joyously drunk in the presence of women they respected. For in the outlying desert regions where I had lived this was not done. Partly because of this novelty and partly because I myself had developed a psychological and physiological resistance to alcohol far in excess of its reported delights, I gave myself with enthusiasm to discovering what the others got out of it. That it was for Sterling the apparatus by which all his energies were stepped up to the creative level there is no manner of a doubt. By what slip of inheritance he found himself stripped of that natural alternation of psychic levels, which enables some men to pride themselves on their virtue, who can say?

Always he was ridden by restless impotencies of energy, which only by sharp exaggeration of sensation would find their natural outlet in creative expression. He could not give himself either to composition or to intellectual exposition of an idea, nor even sit and lounge comfortably, until by one of three ways his genius had been eased into its appropriate path. When he had been plunging about for an hour in the stinging surf, or wrestling pine knots with an ax, or pounding abalone which had just been strenuously gathered from the rocks, or had several drinks in him—then would talk pour from him gloriously. Striding through the woods at a long-legged pace that few could follow, as one could see him of afternoons, tramping the hills in company with Jimmy Hopper, Sterling's tall figure always a little in advance, had the same high effect on him.

It was the same pagan lack of perception of certain widely human aspects of reality that induced the manner of Sterling's death. For death was to him the dark mother, in which life finds only the relief of oblivion. As there was no capacity in him to conceive the less personal plane of existence, so he failed of realizing the validity of experience unrelated to the pain-pleasure principle by which he lived. He knew nothing whatever of the plane of mystical, creative capacity, to which neither cup nor kiss could lift him. For periods of years, when I knew him, he was never without the means of death, of which he feared nothing but that he should come to fear it. He had a dread of living on until age or disability should rob him of the power to lay down his life of his own volition. He had at times a touch of morbid fear that he should sometime come to suffer pain, though, so far as I ever knew, he had no ailment but youth incurable. What I have said here was what it was agreed among us three that I should sometime say. Withal, he had this abiding virtue, that he lived so sincerely with himself and so vitally that even his failings were contributive and informing.

Much that got into the press about affairs at Carmel had no more fidelity to fact than an item reported by a recent visitor there, in a guide book, to the effect that my house at Carmel had a cow's tail for a bell-pull. The truth is that my bell-pull was a strand of ancient Spanish hair rope, at the other end of which hung a bell which the rope had once supported around the neck of the bell-camel that came with the herd imported by Jefferson Davis for domestication in the American desert. The bell was of bronze, and bore an inscription in Arabic to keep off the evil eye. It had been given me by the *major domo* of the man who had carried the news of the discovery of gold to Washington in '49. This reduction of an article of authentic use and beauty to an absurdity is symbolic of the major misapprehension of Americans in general as to the inwardness of the artist life. There were a good many such, "cows' tails" hung upon the names that made of Carmel-by-the-Sea an unforgettable experience.

VI

Time must serve to appraise Sterling's work. As an influence in the literary development of the Pacific Coast, he will always have to be taken into account. His most Keatsian lines are those which were struck out of him by the Greek quality of beauty as it was once on the coast of Carmel:

Landward he saw the sea-born breakers fare
Young as a wind and ancient as the air...

Now the wild lilacs flood the air
Like broken honeycomb...

In the mind of one who knew him, they are inextricably mixed with the beauty that drew them forth—drift-wood fires on the opal-tinted beaches, the sound of a Japanese flute issuing out of the fog- and moon-haunted pines of the Forest Theatre, great spray heads bursting in the violet-tinted air over Lobos. One sees that whatever place in American literature he will finally take—if not the highest, it will surely be not a low one—Sterling himself will become a myth there, a figure of man noble, inconsequent, but never utterly denied his desire to identify himself with truth and beauty.

from *Earth Horizon*

Book IV, Chapter IV

The country through which these visits to my mother were made was the strip of almost pure desertness which skirts the Sierras, curving west to meet the Coast Range around the southern end of the San Joaquin. There is a shorter way through the Sierras by Walker's Pass, open only in summer weather, but at all seasons the ancient thoroughbrace stage-coaches rocked steadily by eighteen-mile relays from Keeler, at the head of Owens Lake, to Mojave, on the Southern Pacific, which carried one back on the track to Bakersfield. If one happened not to know enough to engage in advance the seat beside the driver, the trip was rather a horror, crowded into the stuffy interior between "oldtimers," liquor salesmen, mining experts, an occasional stray "girl" from the local bawdy-house, or one of those distressed and distressfully pitiable "lungers" of whom you had the grace only to hope that he wouldn't die on your shoulder. Outside there was a magnificent panorama and often very good entertainment. Among purveyors of story material, stage-coach drivers bear the palm. Mary was always able to secure the outside seat. No matter how many times she had been over the road, she was always ready to hear the tale again and could give story for story, besides being well provided with baskets of fruit and chocolate layer cake and such-like comestibles as while away the midnight hours, for the trip was always made of one continual stretch of twenty-six hours, with eighteen-mile relays. I have incorporated so many of those tales into "Lost Borders" and "One Smoke Stories," that there

is little left but that inconclusive sort of actual incident of which
the point is always that of your being there for it to happen to. I
recall once setting out for Mojave at such an hour that midnight
brought us to Red Rock Canyon, one of the weirdest wind-sculp-
tured defiles of the West, with nobody on board but three or four
nondescript male passengers and Mary on the boot beside the driver. Where we slowed down by the drag of the wind-sifted sand in
the dark of the canyon, a figure moved mysteriously up on our
right...the driver laid his hand warily on his hip and the stranger
hastened to make known his quest...

"Ye got anybody on board that can pray out loud?"

The driver halted, gun-hand squared to the stranger's direction.
Nothing came out of the interior but the sound of heavy breathing.

"We got a man here's pretty badly hurt," apologized the inter-
locutor; "he'd like to have somebody pray for him."

After another dead interval, Mary leaned across the driver's knee.
"I could pray," she said.

The dark stranger peered and hesitated. "You're a lady, ain't ye?
The man's pretty bad—"

"I got the mail," the driver explained; "I could wait fifteen minutes."

Mary began to clamber down in the dark.

"Here you," the driver called indignantly into the interior, "ain't
some o' you fellows goin' with the lady?"

Grunting, two male figures took form in the mitigated dark of
the stage lantern; we followed the stranger around a coign of the
canyon wall. There was a camp there and a low fire; a wagon bulked
darkly and beside the fire the hurt man propped on a bedding roll
under a blanket. "Here's a lady come to pray with you, Bill." Bill was
evidently far gone. He tried to speak; tried to push back the blanket,
which showed him bandaged about the breast. Another man came
up from the wagon, carrying one of his arms awkwardly, muttering
something. The guide put the blanket firmly back. "Don't keep the
lady waiting, Bill." Mary caught the wandering feeble hands of the
hurt man in hers... "Merciful Father..." she began; behind her she
could see, or rather hear the standing men taking off their hats.
There had been, Mary considered, some sort of a shooting

scrap…no time to think of that… "Repeat after me: Christ Jesus, forgive my sins…" "Jesus…forgive," very faint; "and receive my spirit…"

When we got down at Keeler the next afternoon, the two men who had stood behind Mary when she prayed came up solemnly and shook her by the hand. Later the driver told me that on his daylight trip back he had stopped long enough to visit the death camp, but besides the cold ashes he found no trace.

Things had a way of happening at Red Rock. It was there Mary came upon an altar once, and a priest saying mass to three herders kneeling among their silly sheep…and there she saw the ghost of Vasquez' horse; Tiburcio Vasquez, the most popular bandit… "He stole from the rich and he gave to the poor." And after his death the horse used to go over and over the accustomed route looking for his master, in life, and regularly after it became a ghost… (That's not the only ghost horse seen in the West.) Vasquez used to keep a lookout on the tall rock above Coyote Holes for the bullion teams out from Indian Wells, and to make a signal smoke. There was a story at Coyote Holes—but I've written that.

Once—but whether it was later or earlier I forget—there was a woman at Coyote Holes that interested Mary greatly. She was a middle-aged school teacher from Vermont, or perhaps Connecticut, who had come out under the protection of a matrimonial bureau to marry the keeper of the stage station. He was middle-aged too, and had been known as the Bad Man from Bodie— Bodie you'll find in Mark Twain's account. Mary used to see that sign—Water, Hell, or China—when she went that way, and always meant to possess it, but a high wind blew it away. The Bad Man was reputed to have nine notches in his gun, but after fifty years he began to yearn for respectability and the peace and pleasantness of his mother's home in New England; hence the resort to the matrimonial bureau. Mrs. Bodie, as we will call her, came on and married him sight unseen at Mojave. She brought braided rugs and a melodeon, and planted hollyhocks in the station yard. Mary used to bring her geranium slips and saved seeds. She said she was perfectly happy, but missed her church privileges. Bodie did what he could to make it up to her. Sundays he shaved and put on a clean shirt, and the two of them sat on the porch rocking and singing Gospel Hymns. She never knew that he had been called the Bad Man from Bodie.

Mary saw more than a few matrimonial agency marriages in the old West; they turned out on the whole as well as other people's; where no deception had been practiced, often more satisfactorily. There were instances, of course, that were ludicrously pitiful...meager, defeated souls tricked out for the dance of ecstasy recaptured, looking out aghast, from their wigs and paint, at what they saw of themselves in the other.

Several adventures of the Mojave stage-coach couldn't have happened to anyone else. Mary always took it going south or to the San Joaquin Valley, "over beyond" as the phrase was. For getting "down below," which meant anywhere about the Golden Gate, one took the narrow-gauge on one of its three weekly trips, connecting with the transcontinental lines at Reno. There were peaks in Inyo from which it was solemnly averred by people who had climbed them that ships could be seen going in and out of the Bay. The narrow-gauge was slow enough, as railroads were estimated, and once they stopped on the Divide for Mary to make a snow man, and at Walker Lake, when there were no ladies aboard, for the train men to take a swim; but you couldn't hop on and off to pick strange flowers, nor hold up the train while the station keeper at Black Rock finished a long-drawn gruesome tale of a traveler going out with his "pile," who was killed there and fed out to the passengers as pork, so that his ghost, in the form of a large black pig, took to haunting the place about meal time. And of course you couldn't have taken the train in, as you did the stage once, when, with nobody in it but an English mining expert going to Indian Wells and Mary with her baby, the driver tried to turn round about halfway between Mojave and the eighteen-mile house. He said he was sick because the water of Mojave hadn't agreed with him, and passed out. Mary and the Englishman contrived to double him up and project him in that condition onto the front seat, and the mining expert, who professed to know nothing of horses, held the baby while Mary strapped herself to the boot and took the stage in to the eighteen-mile house. We were late, of course, and it was several days before Mary got the stiffness out of her arms, but it was great fun. A dozen years later, dining at that place in London where they do you so marvelously with hot and cold joints trundled about on a gigantic tea-wagon— Simpson's, wasn't it? and it would have been the Hoovers who took me there—the mining man recognized me and recalled the incident to memory.

There were still a few mines going far out, toward what a few years later became the Johannesburg-Rhyolite district, who got their mail at the Mojave-to-Keeler stage stations, some of them doing assessment work merely, and, in rare intervals of uncovering rich leads, piling up double and triple shifts. This would have been about 1900—exact dates for that period are impossible for me to recover—and by this time Mary was a well-known and somewhat dramatic figure whose passing made a stir. Lonely men in remote stations, men who had not seen their own womenkind in months, when they heard of it, would get into the stations just for the sake of the half-hour's chat with her while meals were eaten and horses changed. On one of these occasions she found waiting for her a pleasant-looking man, superintendent from let us call it the Lost Burro Mine—there was one of these in every district—who said openly, before everybody, that his old mother was out at the mine with him, hungering for women's company; would Mary go out and spend a day with her? The plea was valid for the time and country; Mary had always wanted to see the Lost Burro, and, as it happened this was one of the few times when she did not have her daughter with her, the stage-coach could pick her up at the same place the day after. It wasn't until they were four hours on the road that Mr. Burro, so we will call him—he did make something of an ass of himself—began to exhibit great uneasiness. His mother, he confessed, was safe in her home in Philadelphia; he had cooked up that yarn to save my face with the station people. The boys, he said, meaning his staff, assayer, foreman, and accountant, had been taken with the idea of having a visit from Mary, and he had been appointed to arrange it. Could she possibly forgive him and go on with it? That was where he showed himself most asinine, since simply to have driven out in the desert and to have returned in the middle of the night would have been incredible. The adventure had to be gone through with.

"Who else knows that I am expected?"

"By this time, probably everybody."

"And you know what they will do to you if I tell them I have been insulted?"

He knew well enough; the mining gesture of chivalry is high, wide, and handsome.

"Well, I *will* tell them that," said Mary, "unless you do exactly as I tell you from now on."

The "boys" were all out to welcome the lady—they could have seen us coming for an hour up the grade—including the four China-boy cooks, all stiffly starched and with new green and cerise tassels on their pigtails. They had made in her honor all six of the American desserts they knew, three of which proved to be bread pudding. After dinner, all three of the shifts—the graveyard shift for that occasion had been omitted—all shaved and clean-shirted, came up to have a look at The Lady. They found her with the staff on the long platform that ran the length of the mess-house, in full sight of the camp and each other, with all the implications of constituting themselves a guard of honor. The miners were mostly Cornishmen, with short backs, legs wide apart and lithe but bulging muscles. Two or three had their wives with them, childless women who made a footing in these predominantly male communities by doing laundry and mending. At the very last, two or three other women edged in a little cluster by themselves, to whom everybody pointedly paid no attention. The evening entertainment included cowboy songs, Spanish *canciones* with guitar accompaniment, frontier ballads, such as "Sam Bass," and about the "dirty coward who shot Mr. Howard and laid Jesse James in his grave." Two men danced what was probably once a sword dance. The foreman and accountant did the quarrel of Brutus and Cassius, which was much appreciated. Somebody else did card tricks. Then The Lady recited poetry, something of her own, after which there were sentimental songs with choruses. The Lady made, about eleven o'clock, a dramatic withdrawal that would, I am sure, have done credit to Mrs. Siddons, after which most of the songs were sung over as a serenade. The next morning she was shown ceremoniously over the mine and driven back to meet the stage by a relieved and humble superintendent. It wasn't, however, an adventure that Mary talked much about.

All told, I have had little travel in my life which has yielded so much profit on the exertion as the old Mojave stage. I understand that the road is well furnished now with gas stations and hot-dog stands, and the trip can be made in a few hours without incident. Which seems on the whole a pity.

Major Works by Mary Austin

(in order of publication)

The Land of Little Rain (1903)
The Basket Woman (1904)
Isidro (1905)
The Flock (1906)
Santa Lucia (1908)
Lost Borders (1909)
Outland (1910) [pseudonymously as Gordon Stairs]
The Arrow-Maker (1911)
Christ in Italy (1912)
A Woman of Genius (1912)
The Green Bough (1913)
The Lovely Lady (1913)
California, the Land of the Sun (1914) revised as *The Lands of the Sun* (1927)
Love and the Soul Maker (1914)
The Man Jesus (1915) revised as *A Small Town Man* (1925)
The Ford (1917)
The Trail Book (1918)
The Young Woman Citizen (1918)
No. 26 Jayne Street (1920)
The American Rhythm (1923)
The Land of Journey's Ending (1924)
Everyman's Genius (1925)
The Children Sing in the Far West (1928)
Taos Pueblo (1930)
Experiences Facing Death (1931)
Starry Adventure (1931)
Earth Horizon: An Autobiography (1932)
One-Smoke Stories (1934)
Mother of Felipe and Other Early Stories (1950)
Cactus Thorn (1988)
Mary Austin's Southwest: An Anthology of Her Literary Criticism (2005)

About the Editor

Kevin Hearle is a fifth-generation Californian. He grew up in Santa Ana, where one of his maternal great-great-grandfathers was the first doctor. After earning his bachelor's degree in English from Stanford University, Hearle went on to the Writers' Workshop at the University of Iowa for an M.F.A. and then the University of California, Santa Cruz, for an M.A. and Ph.D. in literature. He has been a founding member of the editorial boards of three journals dedicated to the life and works of John Steinbeck, and he received the Burkhardt Award as the Outstanding Steinbeck Scholar of 2005. He was the revision editor for the second edition of *The Grapes of Wrath: Text and Criticism* (Penguin, 1997) and coeditor of *Beyond Boundaries: Rereading John Steinbeck* (University of Alabama, 2002). His *Each Thing We Know Is Changed Because We Know It, and Other Poems* (Ahsahata Press, 1994) was a finalist for the National Poetry Series. Poems from that book have been included in numerous anthologies, including *Unfolding Beauty: Celebrating California's Landscapes* (Heyday Books, 2000); *California Poetry: from the Gold Rush to the Present* (Heyday Books, 2003); and *The Poetry Cure* (Bloodaxe Books, 2005). Hearle has taught at the University of Iowa, Coe College, UC Santa Cruz, San Jose State University, California State University at Los Angeles, UCLA Extension, UC Santa Cruz Extension, Santa Clara University, and Notre Dame de Namur University. He is one of the regular and founding voices of the public radio program "Your California Legacy." He lives in San Mateo with his wife, Libby.

A California Legacy Book

Santa Clara University and Heyday Books are pleased to publish the California Legacy series, vibrant and relevant writings drawn from California's past and present.

Santa Clara University—founded in 1851 on the site of the eighth of California's original twenty-one missions—is the oldest institution of higher learning in the state. A Jesuit institution, it is particularly aware of its contribution to California's cultural heritage and its responsibility to preserve and celebrate that heritage.

Heyday Books, founded in 1974, specializes in critically acclaimed books on California literature, history, natural history, and ethnic studies.

Books in the California Legacy series appear as anthologies, single author collections, reprints of important books, and original works. Taken together, these volumes bring readers a new perspective on California's cultural life, a perspective that honors diversity and finds great pleasure in the eloquence of human expression.

Series editor: Terry Beers
Publisher: Malcolm Margolin
Advisory committee: Stephen Becker, William Deverell, Charles Faulhaber, David Fine, Steven Gilbar, Ron Hansen, Gerald Haslam, Robert Hass, Jack Hicks, Timothy Hodson, James Houston, Jeanne Wakatsuki Houston, Maxine Hong Kingston, Frank LaPena, Ursula K. Le Guin, Jeff Lustig, Tillie Olsen, Ishmael Reed, Alan Rosenus, Robert Senkewicz, Gary Snyder, Kevin Starr, Richard Walker, Alice Waters, Jennifer Watts, Al Young.

Thanks to the English Department at Santa Clara University and to Regis McKenna for their support of the California Legacy series.

CALIFORNIA
LEGACY

Other California Legacy Books

Essential Muir *Edited with an Introduction by Fred. D. White*

Essential Saroyan *Edited with an Introduction by William E. Justice*

The Land of Orange Groves and Jails: Upton Sinclair's California
Edited by Lauren Coodley

Merton of the Movies *Harry Leon Wilson*

Unsettling the West: Eliza Farnham and Georgiana Bruce Kirby in
Frontier California *JoAnn Levy*

Gunfight at Mussel Slough: Evolution of a Western Myth *Edited by Terry Beers*

California Poetry: From the Gold Rush to the Present *Edited by Dana Gioia, Chryss Yost,
and Jack Hicks*

Indian Tales *Jaime de Angulo*

Mark Twain's San Francisco *Edited with a New Introduction by Bernard Taper*

Storm *George R. Stewart*

Dark God of Eros: A William Everson Reader *Edited with an Introduction by Albert Gelpi*

920 O'Farrell Street: A Jewish Girlhood in San Francisco *Harriet Lane Levy*

Under the Fifth Sun: Latino Literature in California *Edited by Rick Heide*

The Journey of the Flame *Walter Nordhoff*

California: A Study of American Character *Josiah Royce*

One Day on Beetle Rock *Sally Carrighar*

Death Valley in '49 *William Lewis Manly*

Eldorado: Adventures in the Path of Empire *Bayard Taylor*

Fool's Paradise: A Carey McWilliams Reader *Foreword by Wilson Carey McWilliams*

November Grass *Judy Van der Veer*

Lands of Promise and Despair: Chronicles of Early California, 1535–1846
Edited by Rose Marie Beebe and Robert M. Senkewicz

The Shirley Letters: From the California Mines, 1851–1852 *Louise Amelia Knapp
Smith Clappe*

Unfinished Message: Selected Works of Toshio Mori *Introduction by Lawson Fusao Inada*

Unfolding Beauty: Celebrating California's Landscapes *Edited with an Introduction by
Terry Beers*

If you would like to be added to the California Legacy mailing list, please send your
name, address, phone number, and email address to:

California Legacy Project
English Department
Santa Clara University
Santa Clara, CA 95053

For more on California Legacy titles, events, or other information, please visit
www.californialegacy.org.

Heyday

Since its founding in 1974, Heyday Books has occupied a unique niche in the publishing world, specializing in books that foster an understanding of the history, literature, art, environment, social issues, and culture of California and the West. We are a 501(c)(3) nonprofit organization based in Berkeley, California, serving a wide range of people and audiences.

We are grateful for the generous funding we've received for our publications and programs during the past year from foundations and more than 300 individual donors. Major supporters include:

Anonymous; Anthony Andreas, Jr., Arroyo Fund; Barnes & Noble bookstores; Bay Tree Fund; S.D. Bechtel, Jr. Foundation; California Council for the Humanities; California Oak Foundation; Candelaria Fund; Columbia Foundation; Colusa Indian Community Council; Federated Indians of Graton Rancheria; Wallace Alexander Gerbode Foundation; Richard & Rhoda Goldman Fund; Evelyn & Walter Haas, Jr. Fund; Walter & Elise Haas Fund; Hopland Band of Pomo Indians; James Irvine Foundation; George Frederick Jewett Foundation; LEF Foundation; David Mas Masumoto; Michael McCone; Middletown Rancheria Tribal Council; Gordon & Betty Moore Foundation; Morongo Band of Mission Indians; National Endowment for the Arts; National Park Service; Poets & Writers; Rim of the World Interpretive Association; River Rock Casino; Alan Rosenus; San Francisco Foundation; John-Austin Saviano/Moore Foundation; Sandy Cold Shapero; Ernest & June Siva; L.J. Skaggs and Mary C. Skaggs Foundation; Swinerton Family Fund; Victorian Alliance; Susan Swig Watkins; and the Harold & Alma White Memorial Fund.

For more information about Heyday Institute, our publications and programs, please visit our website at www.heydaybooks.com.